Charleston Century

Almost Heaven
1900-1999

STEPHEN H. PROVOST

"Towns change; they grow or diminish, but hometowns remain as we left them."

Jayne Anne Phillips,
Novelist

The State Capitol building in Charleston, seen from across the Kanawha River. *Author photo*

Introduction

Ever since I heard John Denver refer to West Virginia as "almost heaven," the state has intrigued me, so Charleston, being the largest and capital city, was a natural for this series.

The state has a distinctive beauty to it that's unlike any other. Its mixture of meandering rivers, rolling hills, and lush greenery is unlike almost any other.

And then, there's the history.

As you drive into Charleston on U.S. Highway 60, you can't miss the sight of the Capitol dome. It's every bit as majestic as the Capitol building in D.C., but it's even more spectacular when the sun is shining. Its rays reflect off the golden dome and the

Kanawha River in the foreground, creating a glorious scene that's sure to widen the eyes of any first-time visitor. I know it did mine.

Charleston is the first state capital I've covered in this series of books on small and midsized American cities and towns, and with a population of about 45,000 at this writing, it fits perfectly into that category. It once was home to almost twice as many people: nearly 86,000 in the 1960 census. But financial hardship and a decline in the energy and manufacturing industries that once fueled the city's economy have taken their toll.

There is, of course, a lot more to Charleston's story than its role as the state capital. In fact, the city has so many interesting tales to tell that this book has turned out to have more information than a number of other books in this series.

As a sports fan, one of the first things I heard about it was a bit of obscure trivia concerning a football team called the Charleston Rockets that played during the 1960s in the Continental Football League. The Rockets were so good during their first season in the league that they went undefeated, going 14-0 and winning the championship seven years before any team in the NFL accomplished that.

Charleston's also the birthplace of the nation's petrochemical industry. An oil field near Cabin Creek supplied the raw material that made the Pure Oil company a leader in the field. And speaking of Cabin Creek, you have heard of a certain basketball player who went to high school there. Jerry West, aka "Zeke from Cabin Creek," became an NBA Hall of Famer, top executive, and the inspiration for the league's iconic logo.

If you've ever eaten at Shoney's — and if you live in this

section of the country, chances are you have — you might be interested to learn that Shoney's got its start in Charleston under another name: the Parkette Drive-In.

Charleston's history dates back to 1794, when the Virginia General Assembly (the region was part of Virginia then) designated 40 acres belonging to George Clendenin, one of the first settlers, as Charlestown in honor of Clendenin's father, Charles.

The area near the city was the site of a Civil War battle, and Charleston became the state capital in 1875. More recently, in 2003, it became home to the Clay Center for Arts and Sciences and has continued to evolve into a 21st century city. *Charleston Century* is the story of what happened in between.

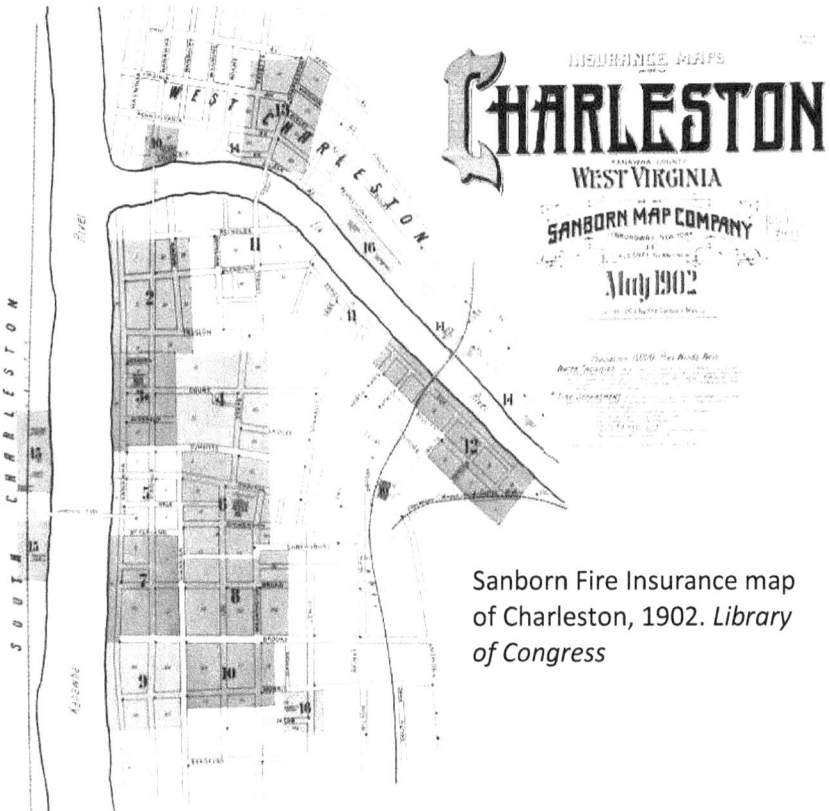

Sanborn Fire Insurance map of Charleston, 1902. *Library of Congress*

STEPHEN H. PROVOST

Diamond in the Rough

1900–1909

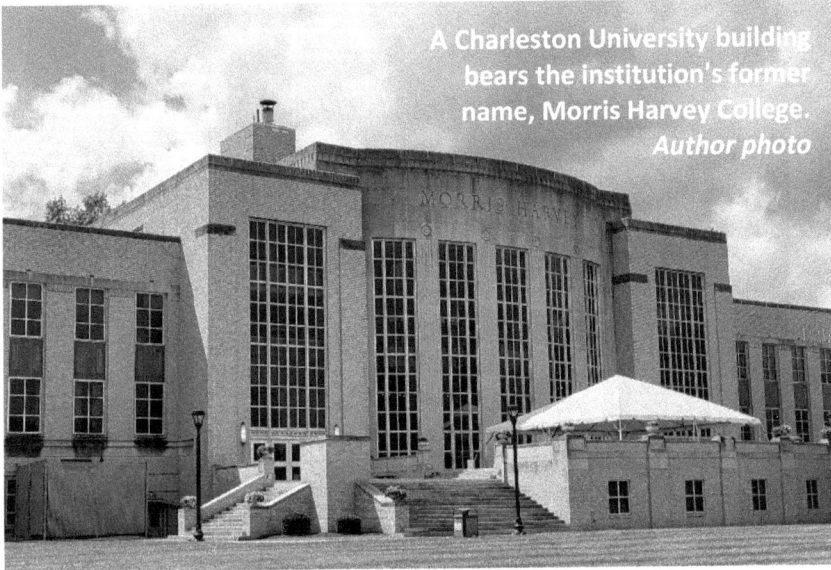

A Charleston University building bears the institution's former name, Morris Harvey College.
Author photo

1900

Business

The Charleston Chamber of Commerce was organized.

Milestones

Charleston's population stood at 11,099, a 64.6 percent increase during the 1890s.

1901

Education

Morris Harvey, a coal operator, bestowed a gift on the

13-year-old Barboursville Seminary, a Methodist school, that helped it eliminate its significant debt. In gratitude, the school adopted the new name Morris Harvey College.

1903

A vintage postcard shows the downtown Arcade in its early days.

Lodging

The eight-story Hotel Kanawha opened downtown, with 96,000 square feet of space. The city's premier hotel — adding a new wing on Summers Street a year after it opened and expanding again in 1917 — and would remain so for almost two decades, until the Daniel Boone Hotel was built.

Presidents Hoover and Roosevelt stayed there, and John F. Kennedy's state campaign headquarters were there in 1960.

The Hotel Kanawha was built right next to the Arcade building, and the fate of the two landmarks would be closely intertwined, as we'll later discover. ...

Retail

The Arcade, with its main entrance on Virginia Street, was already becoming an institution by the time the hotel went up. It was built in 1895 by John Cotton, a druggist, whose brother-in-law, Emmanuel Wilson, had been elected governor of West Virginia in 1884. The building was still in their family eight decades later.

The Arcade was an indoor mall built decades before indoor malls became the fashion. Topped by a skylight to let in the sun, it had a main level and a second-floor, interior balcony lined by wrought-iron railings.

Many cities had arcades in those days: interior throughways connecting two blocks at either end, with shops and offices lining both sides. But Cotton's daughter later said it was the only arcade of its kind in the state, with the closest similar structure being in Cincinnati.

"It was a wonder of the age at the time," she said. "Something for people to walk through and marvel at."

The arrival of the hotel must have been a boon to the Arcade, providing a steady influx of patrons. Charlie Thom's barbershop opened in the Arcade a year before the hotel made its debut, and the business was still operating nearly three-quarters of a century later as Gibbs Barbershop.

The Arcade News Agency would open in 1905, replacing Cotton's druggist, and would be open for at least 70 years after that. The Arcadia Restaurant had its origins as the Virginia Fruit Co. in 1915 and was later called McCarus Confectionary and McCarus Grille. Corey's Arcade Fruit Market opened in 1931.

Other shops that could be found in the Arcade in 1930 included the Men's Value Shop, Arcade Jewelry Shop, Zimmerman's Lunch, Irving's (a women's clothing store), and The Children's Shop. Later additions included Totten Jewelers and The

Dog Wagon.

Merchants came and went, but the Arcade itself didn't change much over the years. Then, along with the rest of downtown, it was dealt a blow when a new-style indoor mall, the Charleston Town Center, opened in 1983. Still, it would survive another 15 years before the end came.

1905

History

The State Bureau of Archives and History opened in Charleston.

1906

Music

The Mason School of Music opened.

Retail

Woodrums' furniture store opened for business on Kanawha Boulevard — which was called Front Street in those days. There were just 22 cars in Charleston at the time. Woodrums' was plural because there were two of them: brothers Charles E. and John R. Woodrum.

The store's made just one sale its first day, a clock, and its inventory wasn't huge: a few rugs and furniture pieces, stoves, and curtains.

But before the year was out, the store was doing well enough to move up the road to a new location at Court and Front. There was a funeral parlor on the second floor, and the third floor was used for storage. Half the first floor was a saloon, and the store recruited its customers to help unload furniture from river barges.

A decade later, the business moved to its final location at Virginia and Laidley streets. An addition at the rear of the store was made in 1936-37, giving the six-story structure 50,000 square feet of space and making it the city's largest furniture store.

Among the store's competitors was "The Great Furniture Store of H.O. Baker Co.," which operated at 901 Quarrier Street for a time. In 1932, it staged a $100,000 "disposal sale" on furniture, stoves, rugs, radios, refrigerators, lamps, carpets, and gas ranges.

Woodrums' outlasted H.O. Baker and the rest of its rivals. ...

Woodrums' furniture store moved to this large building in 1916, a decade after opening in its original location. *Author photo*

The Diamond Shoe Store was founded on the ground floor of a building at 29 Capitol St. By 1914, it had broadened its selection of merchandise to include women's apparel and moved into the first and second floors of a building up the road at 215 Capitol.

By then it would be known as the Diamond Shoe and Garment Company. ...

1907

Cinema

The Wonderland Theater on Capitol Street introduced Charleston to the fabulous world of moving pictures.

Most movie houses at the time were intimate rooms with a few hundred seats. Known as nickelodeons, because admission cost a nickel, so many of them opened that more than 3,000 were operating in 1907, only two years after the first one debuted in Pittsburgh.

Most of them came and went quickly, often opening with a bang and closing up shop a year or even just a couple of months later. But the Wonderland was an exception. It had more staying power.

An early photo of the theater shows a modest building somewhere between 15 and 20 feet wide with an arched single-file entrance on the right and a similar exit arch on the left. A slightly larger arch over a square opening that appears to be the box office occupies the center of the structure, with "LADIES & CHILDREN" written above it.

The Wonderland remained in that location for 16 years and within a year after it opened, it had a new name: the Lyric.

It moved to a new building on Summers Street in 1923, where it would remain for the next half-century.

Journalism

The newspaper founded in 1873 as the Kanawha Chronicle, and later rebranded as the *Kanawha Gazette* and *Daily Gazette*, officially changed its name to the *Charleston Gazette*.

1909

Community

The Charleston Public Library opened its doors.

Retail

The Rogers family sold its drugstore at 612 E. Kanawha Blvd. to Dr. T.B. Stalnaker, who renamed it the Stalnaker Drugstore. In its early history, its customers included the likes of Sam Houston, Henry Clay, and Edgar Allan Poe.

STEPHEN H. PROVOST

Let's Go to Luna Park

1910–1919

A new post office and federal building opened in Charleston in 1911.
Author photo

1910

Baseball

Jack Benny was managing Charleston's first professional baseball team.

No, not *that* Jack Benny. The future comedian was just 16 years old at the time, and he was neither living in West Virginia nor destined for a career in baseball. The Jack Benny in question was present at an organizational meeting of the Virginia Valley League on March 2.

Six cities and towns — Charleston, Huntington, Montgomery, Point Pleasant-Gallipolis, Parkersburg, and Catlettsburg-Ashland — committed to fielding teams. They set a salary cap of $900 a month to keep the larger towns (Huntington, Charleston, and Parkersburg) from buying up all the best players.

The organizers lost no time in getting down to business, setting May 5 as the first day of the season and mapping out a 120-game schedule.

The Charleston team, known as the Senators, would play its games at a 1,200-seat field called Wehrle Park, which had been built in 1908 on land previously used by the Charleston High football team. Batters faced north by northwest toward the outfield, with fans able to watch from a grandstand down the left-field line or bleacher seating on the right-field side.

There was even a set of baseball cards, which came in packages of cigarettes at the time, depicting players from the different teams in the Class D league.

Despite setting that salary cap to ensure a level playing field, the two largest cities wound up with the two best teams. And despite the commitment to a 120-game season, none of the teams played that many, and none of them played the same number, either.

The Senators wound up taking the field more than any other team — and it cost them. Charleston played a grand total of 115 games and won more than any other team: 62. But Huntington, which played just 103 games, won 61, and claimed the championship with a better winning percentage.

Milestones

Charleston's population more than doubled, rising by 107.2 percent to 22,996.

1911

Baseball

The Virginia Valley League changed its name to the Mountain States League, and the Charleston Senators were no longer near the top of the heap.

The team slid down to fifth place in the six-team league with a 57-58 record. Then, the following season, the team disbanded after 40 games.

It wasn't the end of the Senators, though.

Government

The Charleston federal building and post office opened, replacing the old custom house. The building would become home to the Kanawha County Public Library in the 1960s.

1912

Cinema

Joni Mitchell famously sang that "they paved paradise and put up a parking lot."

The Virginian Theatre wasn't exactly paradise, but it was quite the attraction in its day. Built for $20,000 with seating for 700, it opened in October with a selection of four new films.

The Virginian got a major upgrade 10 years later, reopening in November of 1922 with an enlarged capacity of 954 seats, including 351 in the balcony. It had an orchestra pit, and an organist who did more than simply play her instrument: Helen M. Derby supplied her own personal score for every movie.

A detailed terra cotta façade adorned the front facing Lee Street, and the interior décor included chandeliers, marble stairs, and a hand-painted ceiling.

The theater went through a series of owners, joining the Universal Pictures chain in 1926 and switching to Warner Bros. in 1930. Later owners were Stanley-Warner (1951), RKO (1963), and Cinemette (1971), which put drapes over the walls and spray-painted the original ceiling black.

The theater closed in September of 1983 after a showing of the James Bond film *Octopussy*. Plans to convert it into a music hall or dinner theater fell through, and the theater was demolished in 1990, to be replaced by the aforementioned parking lot.

The entrance to Luna Park as depicted on an early postcard.

Recreation

If the name Luna Park was familiar, that's because the one in Charleston wasn't the first. In fact, there were a lot of Luna Parks across the country. You could find them in places as close by as Wheeling, Scranton, Pittsburgh, and as far afield as Los Angeles and Seattle.

The first one opened on Coney Island in 1903 and had

inspired a host of other amusement parks in the first two decades of the 20th century.

Many of them were centered on roller coasters built by Frederick Ingersoll, who opened 44 Luna Parks around the world, creating the first amusement park chain. The parks in Pittsburgh and Cleveland were the first, opening in 1905, and the Charleston park was one of his designs, too.

Like many other amusement parks of the day, it was built along the trolley line, which bolstered both streetcar ridership and park attendance. But people arrived by boat, too, from places like Point Pleasant and Gallipolis.

That's because the park was right on north bank of the Kanawha River, on a seven-acre site that had previously been used for a small golf course.

It had a Royal Giant Dips Coaster that you could ride for 10 cents, or you could visit a zoo on the site (a common feature of amusement parks in those days). There was a roller rink, a merry-go-round, a Ferris wheel, a shooting gallery, and a boxing ring. You could picnic in a park setting or visit the midway.

During the heat of summer, you could cool off in a swimming pool that held 200,000 gallons of water. It was 100 feet long by 45 feet wide, and the depth increased from 3 feet in the shallow end to 8 feet at its deepest point.

Afterward, you could visit the refreshment pavilion for root beer, Budweiser, or Eskimo Pies.

1913

Baseball

The Charleston Senators re-formed and shot all the way to the top of a new league: the Ohio State League. The Mountain States League had disbanded, but the OSL absorbed the

Huntington and Charleston teams.

The pennant race went down to the wire, with Charleston edging out Chillicothe for the crown and Portsmouth not far behind.

Chillicothe had gone into the final day of the season with the lead, but had dropped both games of a doubleheader to Portsmouth, while Charleston took a pair from the hapless Maysville team to win by three percentage points.

Outfielder Cecil Gray had a career season, hitting .366 with 33 home runs. To put that in perspective, no major league player hit that many home runs in a season until Babe Ruth hit 54 in 1920 (having set the big-league mark of 29 the year before).

On the mound, the Senators were led by 24-game winner Ed Hovlik, playing his first season of organized ball, and Al Leake, who went 18-8 in his best season.

The 1913 season turned out to be the high point for this iteration of the Charleston Senators, as well. They'd finish second the following year before posting losing records in 1915 and 1916, moving to Chillicothe midway through their final season. Organized pro baseball wouldn't return to Charleston until 1931, when a new team called the Senators took the field in the Middle Atlantic League.

1914

Cinema

"Charleston's Leading Photo Play Theatre," the Strand, opened its doors in October at Lee and Summers streets, its distinctive corner entrance welcoming movie lovers.

The building also housed The Oriental Shop, which carried Asian goods for women, and (a couple of years later) the Strand Cash Market, which offered "a full line of good things to eat," including meats, butter, eggs, and deli items. "No credit, no delivery, no telephones."

An early postcard of the Strand. *elmorovivo, Cinema Treasures, Creative Commons 2.0*

In 1925, the 900-seat theater was showing what appeared to be an early selection of adult entertainment called *Some Wild Oats.* "Special reels for women only" were scheduled to run continuously from 1 to 10:45 p.m. Friday, and "special reels for men only" were to be shown the following day.

The entertainment, an ad crowed, "shows everything" and consisted of "actual scenes." No children were allowed, and admission was 50 cents.

That was the last ad that appeared in the *Daily Mail.*

The Strand was closed by the early thirties.

Journalism

Former Alaska Governor Walter Eli Clark founded the *Charleston Daily Mail.*

Roller Skating

King Rex was taking his show to new heights.

The daredevil skater was climbing up on the roof of the Charleston National Bank building to perform a "death-defying skating feat" on an 18-inch-wide cornice 100 feet in the air.

Rex appeared regularly at Luna Park. He was known for performing a stunt called the "Slide for Life" there, as well as racing against other competitors. And, as with all daredevils, the risk was the biggest reason for the act's appeal.

When asked about why she'd come out to see King Rex's show, one girl denied wanting to see him crash. But she also admitted the possibility was intriguing: "No, indeed, I wouldn't like to see the skater have an accident, but if he should take a tumble, I'd like to be there to see it."

Luna Park was a big skating venue, and races would continue to be held at the park for the next few years. Race days were elaborate affairs.

Another event during 1914, for example, was described as an endurance race: Stages lasting 15 minutes each began at 9 in the morning, with gold, silver, and bronze medals to be awarded at the end of the day.

The festivities also included fireworks, open-air theater shows, and square dancing.

1915

Basketball

Charleston High School defeated Wellsburg by a score of 36-24 to claim the second annual boys' basketball state championship.

1916

The new Masonic Temple building opened at Virginia and Hale downtown.
Author photo

Community

A new five-story Masonic Temple building at Virginia and Hale opened around the beginning of the year.

Disaster

The sky opened up before daybreak on Wednesday, August 9, and there was no saving Charleston from the near-cataclysm that followed.

The *Charleston Gazette* reported a "cloudburst of immense volume" struck "with the suddenness of a bolt of lightning." Nearly 6 inches of rain poured down in less than five hours near the headwaters of Cabin Creek, which was wound through a narrow valley lined with small mining communities.

One engineer was guiding a 50-car Chesapeake & Ohio freight train along the tracks toward a bridge over the swollen creek. He did as he was told, and it's a good thing, too, because a moment later, the bridge collapsed into the water. In fact, when all was said and done, not a single bridge over the creek remained standing over an 18-mile stretch of track, all of which was destroyed.

The Little Coal River was affected, too. A train bound for St. Albans carrying 210 picnickers from a church group wound up stuck for two days because the bridge over the creek in front of them collapsed. And they couldn't back up because the one behind them was washed out, too.

When the rains finally subsided, hundreds of workers from railroad and coal companies converged on the area along with soldiers and volunteers to search for the bodies of the victims.

Mrs. Woody Jarrell walked 15 miles, carrying her 2-year-old child the entire way, to reach Cabin Creek Junction. The wife of a C&O Railroad engineer had been forced to make the two-day trek without food.

She had watched amidst the downpour from a hillside where she'd sheltered with her child. From there, she'd seen 50 houses, including her own, swept down away by raging floodwaters. All her furniture was lost, along with $250 in cash.

The Daily Mail reported it was the greatest property loss ever seen in the region. Bridges and trestles were "lifted bodily from their supports and carried away." Railroads were "wrenched asunder and their roadbeds undermined."

"Hundreds of houses have been carried away and shattered to splinters, oil wells have been flooded, railroad locomotives and rolling stock have been damaged beyond repair, and numerous mercantile stocks have been swallowed up."

The catalogue of lost property seemed nearly endless.

A restaurant and pool hall were swept away. So were a store and post office. On the left fork of Cabin Creek, 125 houses were washed away as the waters rose at a rate of a foot every 10 minutes.

And lives were lost, too.

One man was able to escape by putting his money in his hat and trying to swim, then clinging to a floating structure until it came to rest against a fence.

A little boy was not so fortunate. He was carried downstream on the floor of a house and lost his life when it crashed into an abutment.

In the aftermath, 200 members of the West Virginia National Guard had gathered a Camp Kanawha in Charleston's Kanawha City area in preparation for a trip to Texas, where they were supposed to help shore up the border against raids by Pancho Villa. Instead, however, they stayed behind to help victims who'd been left homeless by the flood.

They took their tents, blankets, cots, and rations up Cabin Creek to reach the families that had been left homeless there, climbing the sides of the canyon to reach those stranded above the creek.

Twenty-five bodies — including those of several children — had already been pulled from the area around the small community of Ferndale, which had reportedly been "practically wiped out." Floodwaters had swept away the shacks of five miners, and they hadn't been heard from since.

The final death toll on Cabin Creek was 72, and 900 homes were obliterated. The mines themselves were left inoperable, and 3 in 5 miners who lived on the creek left to find work elsewhere.

Roller Skating

A big competition came to Luna Park in Charleston: The world's roller racing championship was held there over eight nights in the late summer.

Education

Charleston High School was built.

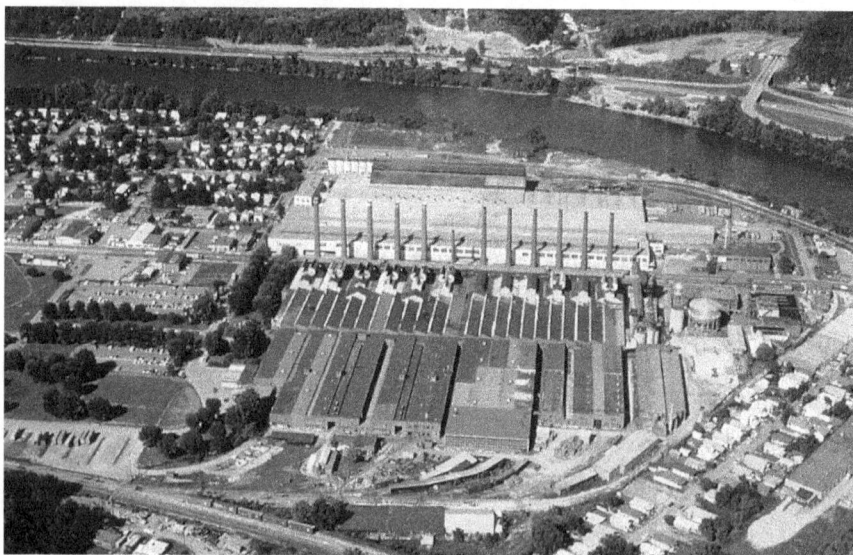

The Libby-Owens Ford Glass Co. factory is seen in 1973. *Harry Schaefer, National Archives*

Industry

The Libby-Owens-Ford glass factory opened.

The company was, at one time, the world's largest producer

of window glass. It provided glass for projects such as the Empire State Building and Waldorf Astoria Hotel. The Charleston plant remained open until 1980.

1917

Cinema

The Rialto at 815 Quarrier St. was unique: It was the only downtown theater that was positioned sideways toward the street. Once you entered the front door, you either turned right toward the balcony — a series of tiers going upward — or left toward the screen.

The Kanawha County Courthouse. *Author photo*

Government

Additions were made to the county courthouse, originally built in 1892. More additions would come in 1924.

1918

Fire

Flames consumed the *Charleston Gazette* building at 909 Virginia St. East on May 18.

Following the fire, the newspaper would move to a new location at 227 Hale St., where it would remain for the next 42 years. *The Gazette* was owned by William Chilton, who served in the U.S. Senate from 1911 to 1917. It remained in the Chilton family for more than a century.

1919

Basketball

Charleston's boys won their second state title by defeating Buckhannon 26-23, but Buckhannon would gain revenge two years later with a 22-17 championship win.

Retail

Piggly Wiggly was making a bid to challenge A&P for supremacy in the corner grocery trade. A&P operated thousands of stores across the country (including eight in Charleston by 1925), but Piggly Wiggly was growing fast.

Clarence Saunders had founded the first store in Memphis in in 1916, and already the new chain had an outlet in Charleston. The first true self-service grocery store, it invited customers to pick up a basket at the entrance and wind their way through the shop until they got to the checkout counter, where they paid for their groceries.

It was a radical departure and, as it turned out, the wave of the future.

The company's Charleston store, opposite the Virginian Theatre on State Street (now Lee Street), asked customers whether they were "paying more than these prices" in a June newspaper ad.

The first item advertised: a small can of Underwood deviled tongue (yes, tongue) for 21 cents. The last: a pound of kippered herring for the same price. Other deals included liquid veneer for 38 cents, ginger snaps for 32 cents, Spanish pimentos for 18 cents a can, and Lux soap flakes for 12½ cents a package. Customers evidently had to buy two of those — or saw a penny in half.

Piggly Wiggly still had a store in Charleston as of 2021, more than a century after the city's first Piggly Wiggly opened its doors. *Author photo*

Pure Profit

1920–1929

Union Carbide's presence in the Charleston area would grow by leaps and bounds over the next few decades. This photo shows a barge at Blaine Island in the Kanawha River. *Henry Schaefer, EPA*

1920

Industry

Union Carbide and Carbon Corp. was just three years old, but its leaders knew an opportunity when they saw it, and that opportunity was just about 20 miles up the road from Charleston in the little town of Clendenin.

UCCC had been formed in 1917 from a merger of five companies: National Carbon, Union Carbide, Prest-O-Lite, Linde Air, and the Electrometallurgical Corp. (Prest-O-Lite, incidentally, was the car headlamp company that had made a millionaire of

Carl Fisher. It was Fisher who built the Indianapolis Motor Speedway, spearheaded development of transcontinental highways, and developed Miami Beach.)

Each of the five companies used calcium carbides to power welding and portable lamps, so it made sense for them to join forces.

The new combined company purchased a small refinery in Clendenin to extract Appalachian natural gas for its products. It began extracting propane, butane, and ethane to sell commercially, fueling the rise of the petrochemical industry.

Milestones

Charleston continued to grow rapidly during the 1910s, with the population rising by more than 72 percent to just shy of 40,000.

Retail

The Diamond had started out as a shoe store, but it was now the city's leading department store, occupying the addresses of 209, 211, and 213 Capitol Street. In fact, it was the largest department store in all of West Virginia, with 200 lineal feet of window space.

Officially branded as the Diamond Shoe and Garment Co., but known to most as simply The Diamond, it boasted that it was "ten stores in one." In addition to shoes and women's wear, it now sold men's wear, jewelry, and toiletries, and there was a complete children's store (including a baby shop and toy section) on the third floor.

The men's store was the latest edition, opening April 17 as "another spoke in the wheel of Diamond progress."

And that was just the beginning.

By 1927, the store would move to a massive building up the

block at Capitol and Washington streets, a site that Artimus W. Cox had coveted for his own Cox Department Store. But Cox's fellow investors had balked at the idea, protesting that the land was too expensive. So he had sought out Wehrle Geary, who operated The Diamond, and they entered into a partnership to build a new Diamond Store on the site.

Geary was, in Cox's words "a very smart man."

"He wasn't afraid. When we went into debt $1,853,000 on the last round of The Diamond, to put on seven floors and an escalator, he was just as cheerful as I was. We had to borrow a lot of money, but Geary wasn't afraid. He was older than I was but not afraid — a smart feller."

The new store, once again the largest in the state, indeed boasted West Virginia's first escalator. At its height, it encompassed 226,000 square feet, including such diverse departments as a tennis shop, maternity shop, furniture center, carpeting department, electronics department, and major appliances center. There was a "bargain basement" in (naturally) the basement, too, as well as a cafeteria on the fifth floor.

The Diamond was particularly known for its iconic corner Christmas window, which displayed a variety of toys and a model train every holiday season.

In 1949, the store undertook a $1.25 million expansion and renovation project that included five elevators and a new set of escalators.

The Diamond would add an adjacent men's store in 1964 and a 100,000-square-foot branch store at Parkersburg's Grand Central Mall in 1972.

Cox's own namesake department store at 222 Capitol St. flourished as well. Cox had purchased the bankrupt Ort's Department Store (slogan: "If you don't buy at Orts, you oughta!") in 1914. And seven years later, it occupied a five-story building with 50 employees and sales of more than $600,000.

A.W. Cox Department Stores expanded to become a chain of 21 locations in West Virginia, Kentucky, Ohio, and Virginia. The Charleston store closed in 1984.

1921

Crime

The young teacher and her class in the tiny town of Decota, south of Charleston, put their hands in the air with their faces to the wall.

Two gunmen had forced their way into the classroom and were firing their revolvers.

At the floor.

At the ceiling.

Clearly, they were not happy. And they'd obviously been drinking. One of them, Floyd Williamson, was a watchman for the Pure Oil Company, which operated the nearby Cabin Creek Oil Field. Before he and his accomplice rode on horseback to the school, they'd gotten into an argument with a clerk at the local YMCA.

When they left, the clerk called the local magistrate to file a complaint. A judge immediately issued a warrant, but before the authorities could respond, Williamson and his companion had crossed the road and barged into the schoolhouse. The teacher and her students managed to survive the encounter, and the two men rode away north toward Leewood, another small community, "firing promiscuously at other pedestrians as they came," according to the *Daily Mail*.

Constable E.W. Williams, a former deputy in Charleston, caught up with them in the residential section of Leewood and told them to put 'em up. Williamson's companion complied, but

Williamson himself reached toward his pocket. The constable repeated his command, but when Williamson went for his revolver, the lawman fired.

The first shot missed, but his second was true: It hit Williamson squarely in the chest. The 26-year-old bachelor died later in the hospital, but not before admitting that he had been reaching for his gun when the constable fired.

The constable was arrested on a technical charge of murder but was later exonerated.

And the children at the schoolhouse had one heck of a story to tell their own kids when they grew up.

Charleston City Hall. *Author photo*

Government

Charleston City Hall was built.

Retail

Young's Department Store opened its doors at 1613

Washington St. West. It would add more space in 1941, with a five-and-dime next door.

A clearance sale in 1963 offered "drastic reductions" of up to 50 percent on a line of dresses, shirts, shoes, blouses, and sweaters. Ladies' blouses, men's dress shirts and sweatshirts, and boys' knit shirts were on sale for 97 cents each.

Young's Department Store on Washington Street. *Author photo*

1922

Cinema

It was, according to an ad, "an Event of Immeasurable Delight."

The Kearse Theatre opened in November on Summers Street between Fife and Quarrier with a showing of Rudolph Valentino in *Blood and Sand*, costarring Lila Lee and Nita Naldi. Adults could attend for 44 cents, and children's tickets were half that price.

"Never before in the history of the theatrical business has a theater opening been attended by such a gathering of statesmen," the newspaper crowed.

Built at a cost of half a million dollars, the expansive movie house had seating for 2,000 people, including 800 in the balcony and the remainder in radial seating on its gently sloping main floor. It had an orchestra pit and was equipped with a large pipe organ from the Austin Organ Company of Hartford; the seats were wider than normal, upholstered in leather and, in the balcony, rose velour.

The Kearse Theatre is visible, with Sears next door. The Greyhound bus depot in the foreground places this photo sometime after 1937. *elmorovivo, Cinema Treasures, Creative Commons 2.0*

A pair of storefronts opened out onto the street from what the owner described as "The Theatre with a Personality." Upstairs were two floors of ballroom space, and club rooms for the Knights of Columbus and B'nai B'rith.

Summers Street was rapidly becoming, according to a story in *The Daily Mail*, the "Broadway of Charleston," with five theaters operating within a single block.

A look inside the Kearse Theatre. *Granola, Cinema Treasures, Creative Commons 2.0*

The Kearse was placed on the National Register of Historic Places in 1980, but notwithstanding this, was demolished a mere two years later. ...

The Grand Theatre opened at 121 W. Washington St. in the Knights of Pythias building, with its impressive second story, two-columned arch. The building, designed by African-American architect John C. Norman Sr., housed the theater for only a brief period, until about 1927. It was later used as a hospital until the 1980s.

Lodging

In 1912, G.E. Ferguson didn't have $5 to his name.

A decade later, he spent $200,000 to realize a dream:

Building a hotel for Black patrons in a building that also included a dance hall, pool room, movie house, café, and barber shop. The so-called Ferguson Block was on Washington Street between Capitol and Broad streets.

Ferguson, 33, was the son of a miner from Montgomery, a little more than 25 miles to the southeast. He'd always been exceptional, becoming a teacher out of high school and graduating first in his class from West Virginia State. Later on, he would identify the site for Wertz Field, the first site to schedule air services in the Charleston area.

The Ferguson Block as seen in an early postcard.

When he got into real estate, Ferguson started out with less than $5, which he'd invested along with three others in a real estate deal. They needed $20 among them but didn't have it; still, they were able to make the deal by having the price reduced to $15. He had continued in real estate from there, making larger and larger deals as he worked his way up.

He took time out to serve in World War I — even though he had a wife and two children to support — and became the first

Black officer to command a troop ship to France. He earned the nickname "Cap" in the process.

"At a meeting of all the officers," he recalled, "I explained that it was the first time I had ever been on a boat, and the biggest thing I'd ever seen was a packet steamboat on the Kanawha" River.

He later organized the first Black American Legion post in the state. But when he attended an organizational meeting for the Legion in St. Louis, he was told to leave the room at the Hotel Statler and was only allowed to remain after West Virginia threatened to withdraw if all its delegates weren't recognized. Hotels in the South were, at the time, segregated.

So Ferguson opened his own.

The Hotel Ferguson opened in March, and was an immediate success. But catering to Black guests was a challenge economically, he said.

"I have to meet the problem of giving the best service for a smaller amount than the white hotels receive," he explained. "A colored man cannot afford to pay as much as a white man, generally speaking."

The hotel had 70 rooms, and Ferguson had to charge at least $7 a week to make it pay. Unfortunately, many Black guests couldn't afford that price, so he put twin beds in some of the rooms and rented them to two men paying half the price each. Each man had a locker in the room to store his belongings.

Each room had hot and cold running water, and some had private baths.

The barber shop was in the basement, and the café was just off the hotel lobby, beside the movie house. The ballroom was at the rear of the lobby, also adjoining the café.

"You see, everything is interlocking," Ferguson said. "Whenever there is a dance here, the dancers step right through this door to the café. On dance nights, the receipts of the café are always heavier than other nights. Guests of the hotel wish amusements, and they go to the moving picture show or the pool room. A man comes to play pool, gets hungry and goes to the café. If he needs a shave, he goes to the barbershop."

Customers outside the Ferguson movie house. *elmorovivo, Cinema Treasures, Creative Commons 2.0*

Ferguson had a dream of expanding his operations to several other cities, ticking off Chicago, Cincinnati, Cleveland, Columbus, Detroit, and Indianapolis. If he could succeed in a place like Charleston, "where there are only about 5,000 colored persons," he reasoned, "don't you think it would be successful in a city where there are 40,000 or 50,000 and no such hotel?"

Two years later, the directors of the G.E. Ferguson Corporation held their first meeting at the Hotel Ferguson, having pulled together $350,000 — the largest amount ever accumulated by one group of Black businesspeople in West Virginia.

Three years after that, in 1927, a judge ordered the sale of the Hotel Ferguson property at public auction to satisfy the claims of creditors. But Cap must have been able to save the hotel, or buy it back, because a 1952 newspaper column once again identified him as the owner.

Ferguson was still high on Charleston at that time.

"Charleston ranks among the top three cities in racial tolerance," he said, also naming Atlanta and Durham, North Carolina, "the reason being the fine spirit among [Charleston's] white citizens, which permits a Negro to walk down the street with his head held up in pride. It's not that way everywhere."

If he had encountered significant discrimination, he said, he "wouldn't have made it to first base."

"After all," he concluded. "Charleston has the largest colored population — about 7,000 — of any city in the state, and I've already told you the reason why."

Retail

William H. Older managed the Fife Street Shoe Shop, where you could get heel taps attached to your shoes and have your hats cleaned, too. There were individual curved booths where you could wait while your shoes were being repaired, each equipped with an ash tray if you happened to be a smoker.

The employees could even solve less conventional problems. One person once asked what it would take to remove dried brown shoe polish from a gold leather stool. The Fife Street folks cautioned not to try it yourself: They could remove it, and if the leather was stained, they could restore the color pretty close to its original.

The store was open at 708 Fife St., at the back of Scotts' Drug Store (an ad in 1962 touted its 40th anniversary). ...

The Charleston Motor Sales building on Leon Sullivan Way.
Author photo

Charleston Motor Sales left their old Virginia Street location for brand new building at 211 Broad St. (now Leon Sullivan Way). The company specialized in Ford and Lincoln automobiles, and Fordson trucks and tractors.

"Our shop measuring 60 by 120 feet is the largest repair and service station in Charleston," an ad in *The Daily Mail* boasted. "Space is provided for as many as twenty cars simultaneously and storage space is provided for twice as many cars. ...

"We will be able at any time to build several cars or trucks complete from our stock of genuine ford parts."

A century later, the building is vacant but still stands. ...

A new four-story Coyle & Richardson Department Store building at Lee and Dickinson was in the works for $175,000.

The business dated all the way back to 1884, and had been at Capitol and Lee since 1908. That building hadn't been small: In fact, it had been a full six stories. But it was long and narrow compared with the one that replaced it.

The new building would open in 1923.

You could get a lot of different things at Coyle & Richardson, including fruits and veggies in their downstairs grocery. You could buy lettuce for 28 cents a pound, a large pineapple for the same price, or a bunch of asparagus... ditto. Peppers were 5 cents each, and celery was 15 cents a bunch.

If you wanted to load up on groceries, you could save yourself a trip: Orders of $1 or more were delivered free.

1923

The People's Bank Building opened on Summers Street in 1923.
Author photo

Business

The eight-story People's Bank Building went up on Summers Street.

Roosevelt Junior High in 2021. *Author photo*

Education

Sacred Heart High School and Roosevelt Junior High (grades 7 through 9) both welcomed their first students.

Fire

A fire torched its way through Luna Park, reducing the amusement center to what one newspaper called a "vast ruin" and a "sodden wreck."

The fire caused damage estimated at $75,000. Most of the attractions were a total loss.

The roller coaster.

The dance pavilion.

The skating rink.

And the swimming pool, which is the area where the fire started. If that seems strange, consider that the pool was made out of lumber and sheets of tin, rather than concrete. The railings around the sides were wood, too, and so was the building that housed the dressing rooms.

The fire happened in early May, just a few days before the park was set to open for its summer season. Workers were getting everything ready when sparks from welders' torches at the pool house started the fire; it spread from there to the roller coaster and then throughout the park. In the shooting gallery, the flames caused a series of explosions as the ammunition was ignited.

Everything was destroyed, even the smaller buildings on the site. And although the owner had insurance, it wasn't enough to cover the full cost of rebuilding.

The park never was rebuilt. Instead, it was bulldozed, and a 95-home subdivision was built on the site, in the area of Park Avenue by the river.

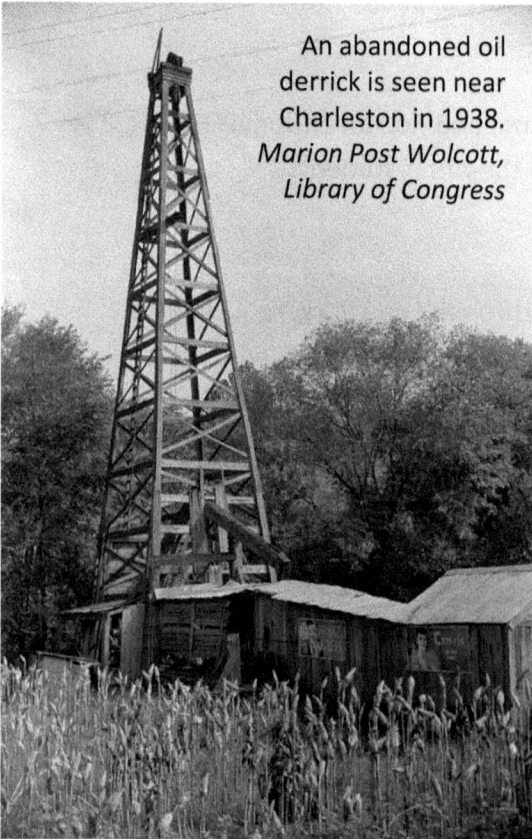

An abandoned oil derrick is seen near Charleston in 1938. *Marion Post Wolcott, Library of Congress*

Industry

Pure Oil was a major gasoline retailer in the Midwest, South and the surrounding region, so it was no surprise that Charleston was adding its third Pure station in September.

The company was growing fast, having been born in 1914 as the Ohio Cities Gas Co. of Columbus, Ohio; it had only just changed its name to Pure in 1920. But it was in December of 1914 that an oil field just 20 miles southeast of Charleston propelled Pure to its earliest success.

That was the first time Pure struck oil in the Cabin Creek Oil Field on the Allegheny Plateau, hitting a daily average of 214 barrels right off the bat. The field would become the largest source of Pennsylvania Crude Oil, producing what the company called "the highest-grade crude oil produced in the country." It would grow to 358 drilled wells on more than 39,000 acres.

Totten's Pure station at Five Corners.
Author photo

Totten's Pure station was located in a prime spot: on a narrow triangular strip at Five Corners between Central and Virginia, facing oncoming traffic on both streets, and cars could enter from either street.

As an added incentive to motorists, the owners offered two free gallons of Purol Gasoline with the purchase of five gallons or more to anyone who stopped at the gas pump on opening day.

1924

Basketball

Charleston High topped Grafton 22-13 to claim the state title for boys' basketball, finishing the season with a record of 23-2.

Track and Field

Charleston High won the first of three consecutive state track and field championships.

1925

Government

The governor's mansion was completed at 1718 E. Kanawha Blvd., across Duffy Street from the Capitol's west lawn. Red brick steps led to an entrance under a high portico supported by fluted white Corinthian columns.

Ephraim F. Morgan was the first governor to occupy the mansion, but he wasn't there long: He moved in just a week before his term expired.

Industry

Union Carbide and Carbon already had a foothold in West Virginia, but that was about to become a stranglehold. In 1923, it bought another plant, in South Charleston, from the failing Rollin Chemical Company. It then built its own facility on the site, which opened in November of '25.

Even with the new space, the company was so successful it rapidly outgrew its new facility. So within two years, it bought Blaine Island, an 80-acre piece of land bisecting the Kanawha River just off South Charleston.

Until then, the island had been used recreationally as a bathing beach, and just before Union Carbide bought it, it was being eyed as the potential site of a tourist camp. Now, instead, it was transformed into what looked like a giant industrial aircraft carrier, outfitted with smokestacks and massive chemical containers — more of which lined the river.

Downriver view of Blaine Island chemical plant on the Kanawha River, September 1973. *Harry Schaefer, EPA*

Lunch hour at Union Carbide in South Charleston, September 1938, *Marion Post Wolcott, Library of Congress*

It became the site of the first commercial plant to produce synthetic alcohol in 1930.

Union Carbide purchased the Bakelite Corp., a pioneer in plastics, in 1939. It soon began producing plastic products such as polyethylene, which was used to insulate radar cables during World War II. By war's end, it was producing more than 100 new chemical products.

The company owned an 11-story office building across MacCorkle Avenue and a 700-acre "Technical Center" campus southwest of the plant. At its height, the company employed 80,000 workers at 100 plants in various places and ranked among the nation's 10 most profitable companies.

It was purchased by Dow Chemical in 2001.

1926

Disaster

It was supposed to be an excuse to get out for some fresh air and witness an exciting event.

A carnival stuntman was about to set his clothes on fire and run under the bridge before plunging into the Big Coal River to douse the flames. But the greatest danger wasn't to the stuntman; it was to the people who had gathered on the bridge to watch.

A crowd of more than 100 people had gathered on the bridge, and the spectators were shifting from the downriver to the upriver side of the bridge after Harry McLean, aka "The Human Torch" had passed under the span. That's when the turnbuckle that held one of the two suspension cables broke, and the bridge came crashing down.

At least 13 people were killed and 40 others injured in the accident. McLean himself, his clothing still ablaze, was buried beneath a number of fallen spectators, but he escaped with minor injuries.

1927

Crime

A guest at the Roma Hotel was awakened around 2 in the morning by the sound of someone on the fire escape.

Then, silence.

For the next 40 minutes, everything seemed normal. But then, suddenly, and explosion rocked by the second floor of the hotel at 809 Kanawha St.

Suspicion immediately fell on Joe Mosle, who'd spent most of the past two years at the hotel. It came to light that Mosle had allegedly been part of an extortion scheme against a certain Sam Spina, whose sister Maria owned the hotel. Apparently, Sam Spina had received an unsigned letter a couple of years back demanding $2,500.

Spina refused to pay.

Maria Spina, however, sought to defuse the situation by handing over $100 to Mosle — whom she apparently had determined was connected with the letter. He delivered the money to "three Italians in a cemetery on the outskirts of Charleston," a newspaper reported.

Nothing happened for the next couple of years, until the night when that explosion sent shattered glass flying out over the river bank and brought police rushing to the hotel to see what had happened.

The source of the blast was found directly beneath Moshe's room, which was also directly above Maria Spina's quarters: It was a stick of dynamite, discovered just outside rear wall on the first floor.

Mosle's alibi was as thin as they come. Police found him in his room, and he told them that he hadn't heard anything — that he'd slept through the explosion. But that didn't check out. For one thing, it was still the middle of the night, and Mosle was standing there fully clothed. His bed hadn't been slept in. And as far as not hearing the explosion, the police had heard it four blocks away.

A pair of revolvers were also found in the room.

Moshe was arrested along with a second man, Sam Partoo, who claimed to have returned to the hotel from a poker game after hearing of the blast. Moshe faced four charges: destruction of property, extortion, conspiracy, and carrying a concealed weapon. Partoo was charged with conspiracy and destruction of property.

In the larger scheme of things, police tied the crime to the remnants of an organized gang of Italian "black-handers," as they were described in the press. These men had supposedly come to Charleston from Clarksburg, where some of their fellows had been hanged three years earlier.

Fortunately for Maria Spina, damage to the hotel was minor other than the shattered windows.

It was not, however, the last time tragedy would visit the establishment. The hotel had been given a new name, the European, by September 1931, when the manager committed suicide with a shot through the temple in hotel basement. Frank Molnar, 60, left a suicide note, written in Hungarian.

Radio

WOBU Radio was on the air.

Charleston Radio Supply Co. owner Walter Fredericks, a local realtor and homebuilder, launched the station at 580 on the AM dial in a bid to sell more radio sets at his store. There was, clearly, not much of a market for radios without a station in town, so Fredericks created one.

The station started broadcasting to Charleston with 50 watts of power in mid-September from studios in the Ruffner Hotel. One of its earliest programs was the *Kroger Half-Hour of Entertainment*, sponsored by the grocery chain. Maytag sponsored another program, and news bulletins from the *Daily Mail* were broadcast at 11 o'clock each day.

Particularly popular was a music program called *The Old Farm Hour*, which featured performers like Bill Cox and the Kessinger Brothers. A yodeler and singer named Willie Tyler made appearances on the program, as well.

Cox, a stationary engineer at the Ruffner Hotel who was known to perform risqué material from time to time, also had a problem with the bottle. Known as "The Dixie Songbird," he recorded roughly 150 tunes during the Depression, including a song called "Sparklin' Brown Eyes" that was later covered by Tex Ritter.

Cox himself never quite hit the big time, though, and he was living in a shack in a Charleston slum just before he died in 1968.

WOBU managed to get back on the air after a fire destroyed its broadcasting studio in 1928, causing $5,000 in damage and injuring Fredericks in the process. But that wasn't the only challenge the station faced that year: The Federal Radio Commission, running short on spots on the dial, allowed WSAZ in Huntington (just over 50 miles away) to share the 580 frequency with WOBU. The two stations operated during different times of the day to avoid any conflict

But that ended in 1930, when WSAZ decided it wanted to broadcast full time and enter the Charleston market by boosting its power. This made eminent sense, from a business standpoint, since Charleston was almost as big as Huntington and a higher percentage of the population there (40.8 percent) had radio sets compared with Huntington (35.7 percent).

Of course, it meant stepping squarely on the toes of WOBU, which led to a "wavelength fight" between the two stations.

WSAZ approached Fredericks, seeking to smooth the way by purchasing WOBU, but Fredericks, in his own words, "point-blank refused." He also refused two subsequent efforts to buy the station, each of which, he said, was accompanied by pressure tactics that included WSAZ's application to the radio commission to double its power.

This could, effectively, drown out WOBU.

Appealing directly to Charleston residents via the *Daily Mail*, Fredericks declared:

"The time is now for the citizens of Charleston to protect

their own interests... With radio frequencies and facilities at a premium throughout the United States, Charleston will never again be afforded a local radio station if Huntington is permitted to arbitrarily force the capital city off the air."

Of course, what Fredericks called Charleston's "own interests" were his station's interests first and foremost.

Huntington interests, however, eventually won out. The Huntington Publishing Company, which owned WSAZ as well as that town's newspaper, purchased the Charleston station, moved the studios to Capitol Street, and changed the call letters to WCHS.

The Huntington company, however, didn't keep the station for long, selling it to John L. Kennedy of Clarksburg in 1936. By the time a new decade rolled around in 1940, the station had boosted its power to 5,000 watts.

One of the station's early promotions as WCHS, in conjunction with the Levin Brothers Department Store, was a flight to the North Pole by a certain Lt. Stark, who planned several broadcasts from there with Santa.

Stark's plane would then return to Charleston, with Santa aboard, as well as "as many of the little Elves, Brownies and Fairies as he is able to carry in the plane."

Upon landing at Wertz Field, "Santa Clause will be rushed downtown in order to be in the parade, headed by the Charleston High School band of 85 pieces." Santa would then stick around all month: He was the guest of honor at a banquet for 100 boys and girls at the Daniel Boone Hotel five days before Christmas.

No word on when he found time to appear at Macy's, but then, that's what miracles are made of.

1929

Baseball

Charleston was fielding a baseball team again, albeit of the semi-professional variety.

The team, like its Class D predecessor of more than a decade earlier, was called the Senators; it was a member of the Tri-State League along with teams from Ashland, Huntington, Williamson, Beckley, and Parkersburg.

Charleston had one of the best teams in the league; the Senators led the standings as of Sept. 16 with a 15-5 mark.

Lodging

With the Great Depression still months away, America was living the high life: 11 stories high, in this case.

When the new Daniel Boone Hotel opened on the first day of February, every one of its 250 rooms was booked. Three former governors and a former U.S. senator attended the black-tie gala to mark the occasion.

The C&O Railroad operated a ticket office in the building for guests who were traveling by train. For those who preferred automobiles, an Amoco gas station was conveniently located right across the street.

The hotel had a newsstand and soda fountain at street level, and if you wanted to do some shopping, Montgomery Ward was right next door. Diners had their choice of a coffee shop or formal dining room.

The $1.25 million hotel would expand with the addition of 89 more rooms in 1936 and grow to 465 rooms in 1949. Other upgrades over the years included the addition of a Governor's Suite, air conditioning, in-room television (black and white in the

1950s) and a large mirrored ballroom.

For a while, you could leave your shoes outside your door overnight and find them freshly shined in the morning, but the practice stopped when shoes started to go missing.

The hotel closed in 1981.

The Daniel Boone Hotel provided the city's most upscale accommodations when it opened in 1929. *Author photo*

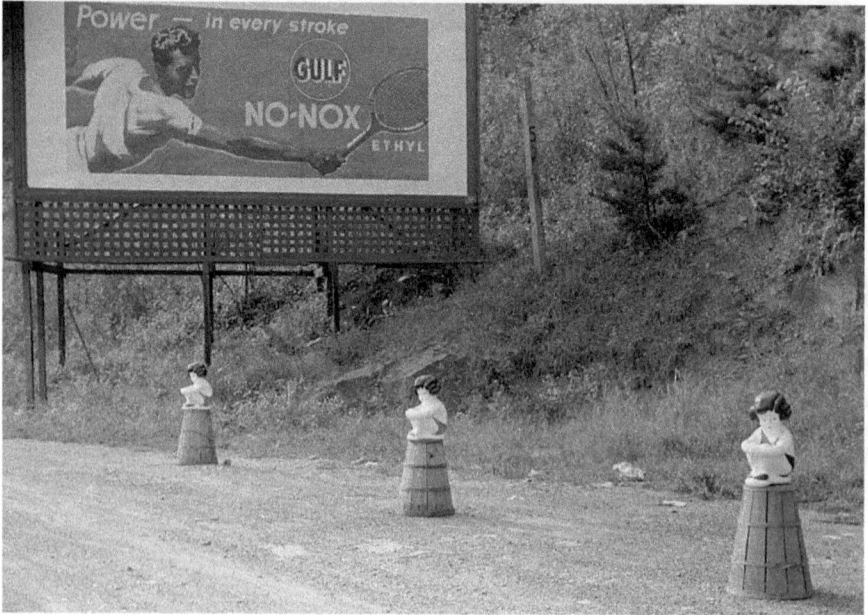

Views coming into Charleston. Kewpie dolls line the road in the bottom photo. *Arthur Rothstein 1939, top, and Marion Post Wolcott, Sept. 1938, Library of Congress*

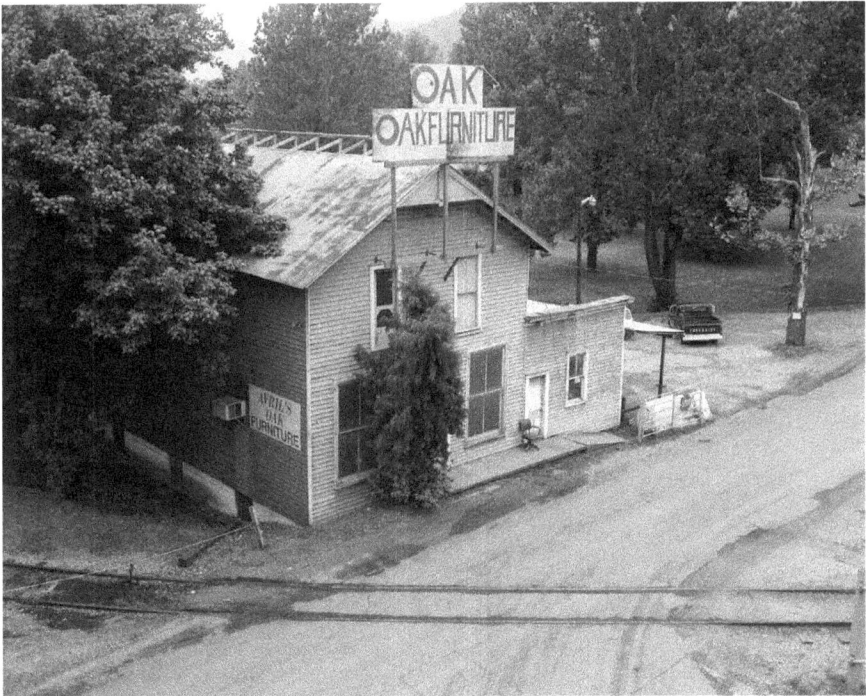

Top: A faded Mail Pouch Tobacco sign on a barn along U.S. 60 (part of the federal highway system founded in 1926) between Charleston and Huntington. *Author photo.* **Above:** Looking southwest at the U.S. 60 bridge at Campbells Creek Coal Co. Store, 54 Port Amherst Drive, Campbells Creek near Charleston. *Historic American Buildings Survey.*

Above: The Grand Theatre building on Washington Street. *Author photo*
Next page: 1920s map of Charleston.

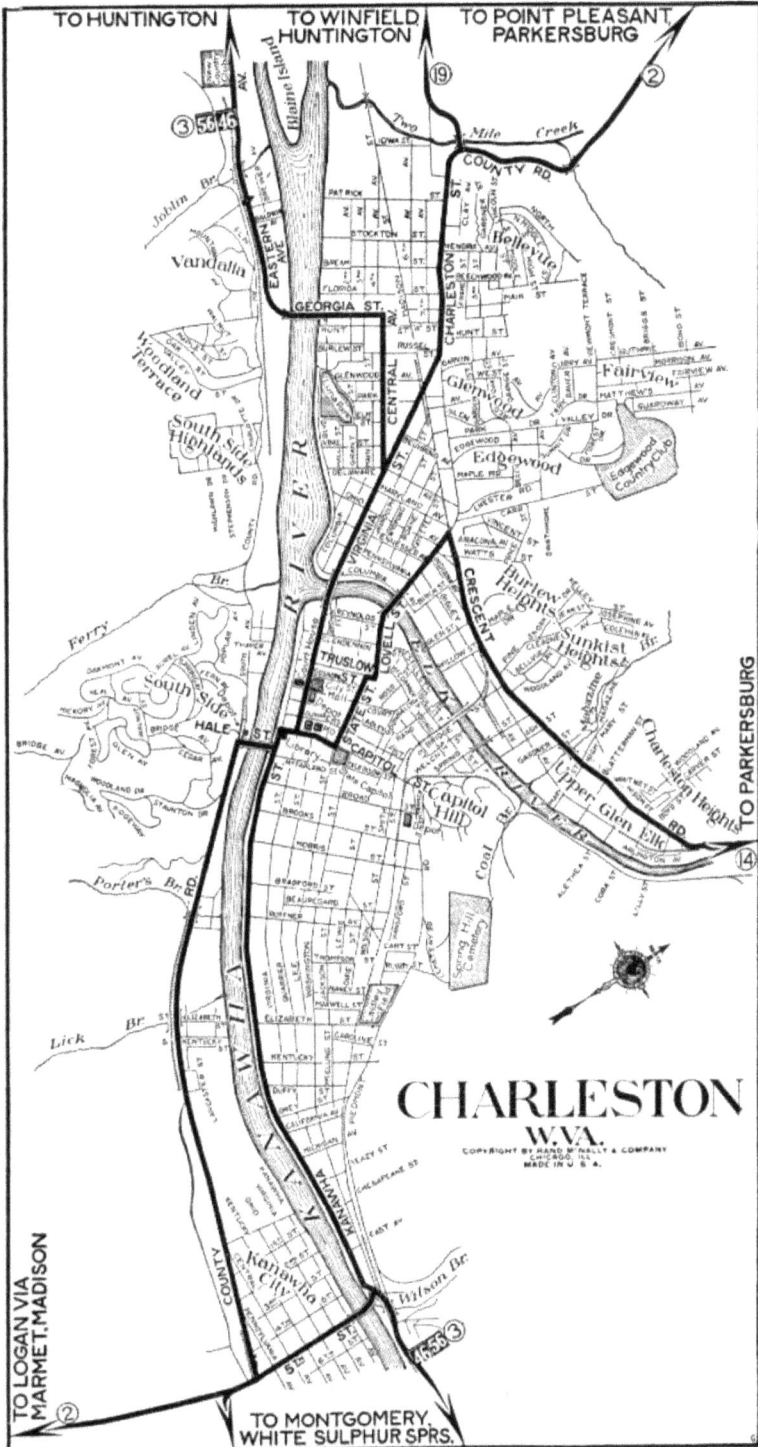

STEPHEN H. PROVOST

Tough Times

1930-1939

A historic Firestone dealership arrived downtown in 1930. *Author photo*

1930

Aviation

Wertz Field opened on Independence Day, giving Charleston access to air services.

"Wertz Field put Charleston on the map for the first time," Christian Hetzel, the first manager at Wertz Field, later recalled.

The new airfield, leased to West Virginia Airways, was named in honor of Charleston Mayor W.W. Wertz. The first commercial airliner landed there in 1933, and by 1935, the field would be used by American Airlines and Pennsylvania Central Airlines. It also offered freight-shipping services.

Technology at the field wasn't what it would later become at airports. Hetzel later remembered being alerted that a plane was approaching via long-distance phone call from Cincinnati or Washington.

"When we saw him, the pilot was ready to land," Hetzel said in 1970. "Those old days of aviation seem unreal when one sees what is happening today."

Wertz Field would host a pilot training program designed to prepare pilots for possible military service. It was home to an early Negro Civilian Pilot Training School, which took in a number of students from West Virginia State, a public historically Black university. Many of the pilots who trained there went on to Tuskegee and World War II.

Wertz Field was closed in 1942 because its runways were too short to accommodate more modern planes. Union Carbide purchased the land, and the city would be without an air terminal until Kanawha Airport opened in 1947.

Baseball

Neither the Charleston Senators nor the Huntington Boosters had advanced to the Tri-State League's "Little World Series" in the circuit's second season. Logan and Beckley had battled for the championship.

But Charleston and Huntington were the two biggest cities in the semipro league, so it wasn't surprising that the Senators and the Boosters were the team to apply for — and be granted — membership in the Class C Middle Atlantic League for the 1931 season.

West Virginia was already well represented in that circuit with teams in Fairmont, Wheeling, and Clarksburg (four of the other five teams were in Pennsylvania, and one in Maryland), so Huntington and Charleston were natural additions. In the end, the Beckley Black Knights joined, too, along with a team from Hagerstown, Maryland, giving the league an even dozen franchises.

Charleston and Beckley both made an immediate impact in 1931, finishing with the best (84-44) and third-best overall records, respectively. The championship series pitted the second-half champion Senators against the Cumberland Colts, who'd won the first half.

The Colts prevailed, 4 games to 2.

Milestones

Charleston's population topped 60,000 after an increase of more than 52 percent during the 1920s.

Retail

The Firestone tire company opened a "one-stop service station" on the southwest corner of Washington and Lee, just the second such store in the nation (the first being in Akron, Ohio, the company's home base).

Charleston was growing fast, and Harvey Firestone expected that growth to continue; C.H. Leesman of the Midland Tire Service Company, the city's Firestone tire dealer, concurred.

"We have received the cooperation of the Firestone company in the erection of the finest type of one-stop service station," Leesman said, "where car owners and truck operators can get complete service for every requirement of operation except mechanical repairs."

You could get motor oil, have your ride washed and polished, receive battery, road, and ignition service, and of course purchase tires at the center.

The store was still there in 2021.

1931

Lodging

You could rent a room at the Jefferson Hotel for between $1 and $1.75 a day. There were 54 rooms from which to choose, and the hotel was conveniently located downtown at Quarrier and Dickinson streets.

Retail

The People's Store, a clothing shop on Capitol Street, was offering a selection of summer shoes in white, black, brown, tan, and other shades for prices ranging from $3.86 to $5.86 — and something else, as well: help selecting a corset from a "corset specialist."

"We know about all kinds of specialists," an ad in *The Daily Mail* proclaimed. "And we consult them when we really want the best possible attention. But how many know that there are corset specialists who you can consult when you want the best possible corset for your figure?

"We're particularly glad to announce that we're going to have a corset specialist in our corset department all week — a specialist who can appraise your figure lines — suggest the correct garment, discuss the mode with you — and send you on your way absolutely content."

1932

Baseball

The Middle Atlantic League, which had fielded a dozen teams in 1931, began the season with half that many — four of them in West Virginia.

Among them were the Charleston Senators, who played their games at 4,000-seat Kanawha Park at 3403 MacCorkle Ave. SE.

The Senators came on strong after midseason to claim the second-half championship and earn the right to face first-half champion Beckley. Charleston (70-54) then earned its first league title by defeating the Black Knights 4 games to 2 in the championship playoff.

Playing manager Dan Boone, who'd spent parts of four seasons as a pitcher in the American League, led the way at the plate for Charleston, compiling a .349 batting average and producing team highs in home runs with 17 and doubles with 30.

Boone would play one more season with Charleston the following year, but the Senators would slip to fifth place in the MAL.

Dining

Brothers Ott and Roma Young had gotten their start working for their great uncles, Clint and Levi Litton, at a diner called the Dog Wagon. Later, they struck out on their own, and had been running the Empire Diner over at 194 Summers St. since 1926 when they bought a new steel diner and plopped it down on a vacant lot at 1022 Quarrier St.

The kitchen was at the far end (with a sign overhead proclaiming, "We don't cash checks"), and tables lined with stools jutted out from either side of the dining car, facing the windows.

The Young brothers touted their Quarrier Diner as "a new

Grill-Type Restaurant" that they considered "the most completely modern dining car in West Virginia."

"It is our aim to provide food of the highest possible quality at all times, and at prices attuned to today's conditions. More — it is our aim to provide surroundings that are pleasing and harmonious to both Ladies and Gentlemen."

The brothers changed the name of their establishment to the Twin Diners when they expanded the place to include a pair of long, attached dining cars four years later.

The Quarrier Diner was closed as of this writing, but it had been a downtown fixture for more than 80 years. *Author photos*

Both were removed in 1946, and a more permanent Art Deco structure was built with seating for 300 customers, as the eatery reverted to its original name.

But the owners had to fight to keep their place on Quarrier Street, because nearby businesses were trying to convert the area into a more upscale shopping district and didn't like the idea of sharing it with a diner. They tried to force the Youngs out, but the brothers fought back by taking their case to the Supreme Court, at the same time personally visiting every business in the area to advocate on their own behalf.

They wound up staying.

The menu at the Quarrier Diner included everything from cheese sandwiches for a dime to 15-cent burgers, and oyster sandwiches for 20 cents. You could get hotcakes, Brookfield sausage, and coffee for breakfast for 35 cents, or waffles with bacon and coffee for the same price.

You could have a porterhouse or fillet steak for just 75 cents, or a T-bone for 60 cents.

New owners took over the diner in 2016, but it was closed again as of 2021.

Fast Food

This part of the story doesn't start in Charleston, but in Mansfield, Ohio, just over 225 miles away. That's where Frank Stewart built the first Stewart's Drive-In in 1924, built around his branded root beer.

He began selling franchises in 1931, and sometime over the next few years, one opened up on opened on Kanawha Boulevard in Charleston, not far from the Municipal Auditorium.

A 1942 photograph showed a cinder-block building with hot dogs priced at a dime. It had a sign over a four-corner roof that advertised three specialties: pop corn (two words), hot dogs, and, of course, root beer.

One thing it didn't have was a ladies room, so the girls and women who worked there had to go next door and use the restroom at the neighboring Parsons Service Station.

The State Capitol dome. The building was completed in 1932. *Author photo*

Government

The State Capitol building with its gleaming dome was completed at a cost of $10 million.

1933

Auto Racing

The Charleston Speedway was a half-mile dirt oval track that hosted auto racing at the Dunbar Fairground. Races were held on July 4 and again on Labor Day, but a newspaper report declared that a poor gate turned the latter meet into a financial failure. Many of the drivers didn't even show up, so organizers settled for a 10-lap event plus qualifying for those who did.

The Dunbar track, originally built for horse racing, hosted midget car meets and motorcycle events at various times during the first half of the 20th century and beyond.

Drivers such as Tommy Ringstaff of Kenova and Owen Spradling of Spring Hill dueled on local dirt tracks like Skyline, Dunbar, and St. Albans in the 1950s. It wasn't NASCAR, but it was competitive, with drivers typically racing in mid-1930s V-8 coupes as they sprinted for the checkered flag.

Spradling, driving a 1934 Ford, won several season titles, including the 1955 crown, and something like 100 main events, going by the credo, "I'd rather wreck than lose." Once, the story goes, he banked his car on the rail to pass the leader and slid upside down across the finish line to win.

That competitive spirit got the former Army boxer into his share of scrapes. One night after a victory, he and his brothers had to fight their way out of Huntington. Police showed up at his housed in the middle of the night with their guns drawn because charges had been filed.

The Dunbar track later closed and became a golf course in the late 1960s, with Spradling trading race cars for a successful welding business. By 1975, he had taught some 3,000 students over a nine-year period in a custom welding class.

One of his jobs as a welder was to create iron gates for the governor's mansion, then occupied by Jay Rockefeller. He sent the state a bill for $450, even though it cost him more than that, but he never got paid. He kept sending the bill again and again, finally getting a response on the fifth try... instructing him to send it yet again, along with four copies plus the original.

"I couldn't believe it," said Spradling, so he sent one of his employees over to do what many business owners in the same position have done:

Repossess his property.

When state police asked him what he was doing, the flustered employee feared he'd be arrested for theft, so he lied and said he was taking it back for repairs.

"I can't run my business that way," Spradling said, declaring, "I don't want the state's business."

And, in fact, he turned down a contract not long afterward to do welding work on a state-owned aircraft. "I told them, 'No way,'" he said.

"I don't care if it is the Rockefellers or the state," Spradling said of the gate fiasco. "If they don't pay their bill, they don't get the gate."

Retail

"Have you driven the new Terraplane?" That was the question the Beane Brothers were asking from their auto dealership at 504 Virginia St. West. The Terraplane was a Hudson product that owed its name to nation's fascination with flying. The first two models reportedly went to Wilbur Wright and Amelia Earhart.

In August, the brothers were offering used car specials including a 1925 Cadillac sedan for $95, a 1931 Ford Coach for $295, a 1929 Essex Coupe for $150, a 1930 Whippet Sedan for $100, and a 1926 Studebaker Duplex for $45.

The Beane Bros. building was a church in 2021. *Author photo*

The building was still an auto dealership in 1967, when it was selling AMC cars like Ramblers and Ambassadors. A new Ambassador was listed at around $3,000 that year at what was then called the Tag Galean dealership.

By the mid-1970s, it was Mountaineer Datsun.

These days, the building is home to a church. ...

Oberlan's was having what it described as its "first and only dress sale," offering 500 summer silk and cotton dresses for just 99 cents and 555 more for $1.99. Summer jackets valued at $2 and $3 were selling for a quarter. All sales had to be cash and in person: no phone orders or C.O.D.'s

The store at 817 Quarrier feared it would be overwhelmed with orders (or so the ad said), because an earlier ad declaring that it would be open until 6 in the evening had depleted its stock and drawn complaints from morning shoppers. So, instead, the store decided to open at 8 a.m. How this solved the problem rather than just moving it around is unclear.

The entrance to Oberlan's on Quarrier. *Author photo*

Newspaper ads for Oberlan's date back to 1915, when the store's address was listed as 234 Capitol Street. In 1933, the Quarrier Street address was referred to as the "Annex." The 1915 ad touted summer dresses for $1.48, so it's questionable whether the 1933 sale was actually the store's first.

Still, the price of 99 cents — nearly a half-dollar lower than it had been 18 years earlier — showed how far things had fallen during the Depression.

Oberlan's would survive the Depression and continue to operate on Quarrier for decades to come.

Track and Field

Charleston High started a four-year run of state track and field titles. The school would win back-to-back titles in 1943 and '44, and again in 1960 and '61.

1934

Retail

Chester's Department Store at 1558 W. Washington St. was holding a holiday bargain event in late November, with ladies' hose on sale for a dime, Turkish bath towels for 12 cents, men's felt hats for as little as $1.49, and men's wool suits for $12.75 or $14.75.

1935

Cinema

The Lyric Theater had a colorful history.

In 1935, it put a 3½-ton sedan "said to have been used at one time by Al Capone" on display outside the theater to promote a movie called *I Am the Law*. The car was equipped with bulletproof steel, quarter-inch-thick glass, and a smokescreen attachment "such as used by gangsters to evade capture."

Capone must have been a good drawing card for the theater, because that same year it screened a Howard Hughes-produced film called *Scarface*, billed as the "true life story of Al Capone."

Five years later, the theater made headlines — and became the target of threats and vandalism — when it screened a movie called *Hitler, Beast of Berlin*. After the title went up on the marquee, theater employees started receiving calls that, unless it was pulled, the theater would "suffer loss."

Sure enough, someone threw a rock through the glass in one of the theater's show cases out front, and three seat cushions inside were ripped open using a sharp instrument.

The manager, Norman Isherwood, did admit that the title was controversial: Theaters in some states had been forced to show it under the alternate title *Goosestep*.

Lyric Theatre at right opened at 140 Summers St. around 1923. It was destroyed by fire in 1975. Note the streetcar tracks. *elmorovivo, Cinema Treasures, Creative Commons 2.0*

But he insisted that there was "no reason for anyone to desire to put a stop to the showing of the film. The title may not meet with everyone's approval, but the picture itself is not in the nature of propaganda — it's just an ordinary feature with the usual romance and dramatic interest."

As to accusations that the whole thing was a publicity stunt, he pointed to the shattered glass out front.

More controversial content would come later, in the 1960s, when the Lyric was converted into an adult film house.

Entertainment

If you wanted to roller skate, you went to the Midelburg Auditorium. If you wanted to hear Jimmy Dorsey and his orchestra, you went there, too.

The auditorium at 1121 E. Lee St. was bankrolled by its namesake, a local sportsman named Charles A. Midelburg, as a venue for circuses, conventions, automobile shows, and large dances. Midelburg referred to it as the "Little Madison Square Garden."

When the Midelburg opened, there were plans to put in a bid to host the 1936 state high school basketball championships. It had enough room in its balcony for more than 3,000 fans, and the auditorium turned out to be the perfect new home for radio station WCHS.

Midelburg sold the venue to the station's owner, John L. Kennedy of Clarksburg, in 1939, and Kennedy changed the name to WCHS Auditorium for a time (it would later revert to its previous name). It turned out to be the perfect place to host the station's broadcasts of *The Old Farm Hour*, which played to crowds of up to 2,000 on some nights.

The most famous name to turn up on the program was Buddy Starcher, also known as "The Boy from Down Home."

Starcher stayed in Charleston for a couple of years during the mid- and late thirties, but would return in 1960 to host his own show on WCHS-TV through 1966. He was best known for a spoken-word record written by Minnie Pearl called "History Repeats Itself" that ticked off similarities between the assassinations of Abraham Lincoln and John F. Kennedy against background music of "The Battle Hymn of the Republic" and "America the Beautiful."

The record reached No. 39 on the Billboard Hot 100, and the album on which it appeared got to No. 37 on the country albums chart.

Other big names to appear at the auditorium during its WCHS years included Artie Shaw and Stan Kenton, both of whom brought their big bands to town.

The station also threw a party at the auditorium for members of the Miss 580 Club, which was the name of a show hosted by

Melva Chernoff, wife of station manager Howard Chernoff. Running for a decade starting in 1938, it featured a phone-in format with advice on relationships, recipes, and other tips, and the annual party drew big crowds.

A family in its houseboat home at Charleston in September 1938. *Marion Post Wolcott, Library of Congress*

Weather

A number of families lived on floating houses on river waters during the 1930s. In January of 1935, high water on the Kanawha and Elk rivers left five of them homeless.

The five houseboats, which were moored near Virginia Street, all sank as the river rose, although others were saved by being towed to higher ground.

These weren't the recreational houseboats we think of today; they were actual floating houses that were homes to families. Not all houses on the river were there permanently. Some were loaded on board barges to be relocated from one place to another.

But a fair number of families actually lived in floating houses. And it wasn't just humans, either. A front-page story in 1933 told the story of how a bantam rooster named Jiggs had tried to jump from his owner's houseboat to shore, only to fall into the Elk River.

But not to worry: The rooster's "best friend," Bill the Duck had come to the rescue, pushing his bill under Jiggs' wing and propelling him to shore.

"It really happened, and it's not the first time," said houseboat owner R.B. Mayes. "Jiggs was flying from the houseboat to the riverbank, but he misjudged the distance. Bill, swimming nearby, rushed in getting him to shore. When I told the story, no one believed me, but it can be proved."

He then re-created the incident, and Bill saved Jiggs... again.

1936

Retail

Today, it's not uncommon to see a Family Dollar, Dollar General, and Dollar Tree store all within a short distance of one another.

The names have changed, but not much else has.

In May of 1936, an ad appeared in *The Daily Mail* showing just how many discount retailers — then known as five-and-dimes or variety stores — could be concentrated in a single block. S.S. Kresge had stores at 209 and 223 Capitol St., while J.G. McCrory was at 218, J.J. Newberry was at 224, Woolworth's was at 205, and H.L. Green was at 219.

Talk about competition.

1937

Ice Skating

R.G. Skinner announced what was hailed as West Virginia's first ice rink at the south end of the Kanawha City bridge, adjoining the Capitol View Golf Course.

The $25,000 rink would be housed in a building with wooden walls and a steel truss roof resembling an airplane hangar. It featured nearly five miles of one-inch pipe to cool the inch-and-a-half-thick ice on the floor, with the water refrigerated using a 38-ton compressor.

You could bring your own skates or rent a pair, and you could sharpen your skates on site. Sandwiches, coffee, and snacks were made in a small kitchen and served at the rink, along with candy, sodas, and cigarettes, but no alcohol was allowed on the premises.

There was a checker's cage along with restrooms and dressing rooms for men and women, and music from record players was broadcast out over loudspeakers.

"The real support we expect to come from the younger generation," Skinner said. "But skating is distinctly not a fad. It is one of the oldest of sports and it appeals to young and old alike."

This wasn't technically the first ice rink in West Virginia because Skinner himself had operated one before — albeit of a temporary nature. In January, he had flooded an area at the Diamond Ice Plant to create a makeshift rink that had drawn an average of 90 skaters a session. That led Skinner to think about something more permanent.

The ice space at his new rink was planned at 180 long by 80 feet wide.

"There are a number of hockey players in the industrial plants, and it is quite possible that games among them could be arranged, to the pleasure of all," Skinner said. "Local instruction and competition should develop expert skaters here within a few years — there are many now — who may rank among the best in the country."

But the ice surface might not have been adequate for hockey, after all, because the rink expanded in 1938, installing bleachers with room for 1,700 spectators and 50 feet of ice space that was specifically added to accommodate regulation hockey games.

Seventy-five new pairs of skates were also purchased for the rink, which was open for two sessions daily: from 2 to 5 p.m. and in the evenings from 7 to 10:30.

Whether skating was a fad or not, however, the rink didn't last very long: It was out of business by 1942.

Retail

The Cox Morton service station began dispensing Keystone gas from Elk Refining on Virginia Street at Goshorn.

Swimming

Rock Lake Pool added a 200-acre picnic area adjacent to the pool itself, with "all new clean tables, a creek for the kiddies to play in, shade trees, and open ground large enough to have a basketball game."

The pool had been open at least since the early 1930s: An ad from 1933 touted a new price schedule, with adults being admitted for a quarter and children for a dime. Swimming lessons were free, and a pass for the balance of the season was $2.

By '37, admission had gone up to 35 cents for adults and a quarter for children, but a host of new attractions made it worth the price. In addition to the new picnic area, there were new water slides and water swings, a new center pier, and sandpiles for kids to play in.

Other attractions at the park over the years included a spraying fountain and trapeze. Swimmers could jump off the platform at the far end and be sent flying into the water when they bounced off a tilted trampoline. There were dressing rooms, and you could get sandwiches and soft drinks at the soda fountain, too.

But the pool itself was the main attraction.

At 530 feet long by 180 feet wide, it was huge, featuring 2.9 million gallons of what the owners described as "pure drinking water" to swim at an old rock quarry five miles west of town in South Charleston. The natural rock walls of the quarry served as convenient platforms for diving. And the park was open from 9 a.m. to 11 p.m. during the summer season.

Ice staking was offered in the winter.

C.A. French and George Caldwell, who had created the pool, sold it in 1942 to a real estate company. Then, four years later, it was purchased by Joe Wilan, who had been managing the property for the real estate company.

Wilan had some experience in the pool business. He had operated swimming hole on the Coal River a mile from St. Albans at Lower Falls Beach until 1931, when he had been forced to close by bad weather during the Depression. Rock Lake Park gave him another shot in the water recreation business, and he made the most of it.

Wilan and his brothers, Sam and Dave, ran the pool for the next four decades. They also owned a variety of other businesses in Charleston, including a restaurant, motel, drive-in, and gas stations.

Transportation

Greyhound opened its new modern bus terminal.

The new Greyhound Bus Depot opened in 1938, as shown in this vintage postcard.

1939

Cinema

The Art Deco style was coming into vogue, and nowhere was this clearer than in the design of new movie houses.

The era of the grand palatial downtown cinemas was at an end, and neighborhood theaters were beginning to spring up in the newly forming suburbs. This trend would accelerate after World War II, but its seeds were already being sewn in the years just prior.

The sleek, streamlined Art Deco style and its close cousin, Streamline Moderne, replaced the gaudy elegance of 1920s movie houses with smoother, curving lines the left you feeling like you were walking through the clouds.

Such was the style in which the State Theatre was built. The 670-seat theater opened in early September and cost $65,000.

The State Theatre building still stands today. *Author photo*

Owners Floyd Price and Gene Custer had just opened the Lewis Theatre in Lewisburg near the Virginia state line a week earlier, and Custer had opened Charleston's Custer Theatre the previous year out on Washington Street.

The State Theatre was still operating in 1961, by which time it was showing adult movies such as *Ritual of Love*. In the 21st century, it's home to the West Virginia School Service Personnel Association, or WVSSPA for short.

Football

The Sportswriters Association named Charleston High state champion.

Community

The fan-shaped Municipal Auditorium, with its central tower facing the intersection, opened on the corner of Truslow and Virginia streets with a seating capacity of 5,000.

The Municipal Auditorium opened in 1939. *Author photo*

Capital Improvements

1940–1949

This Tichnor Brothers postcard shows Capitol Street c. 1940.

1940

Fire

No one knew how the mid-May fire started, but the results were plain to see: The 22-year-old grandstand at Kanawha Park, home of the Charleston Senators baseball team, was destroyed. The loss was estimated at $5,000, with 30 percent covered by insurance.

Milestones

Growth slowed in Charleston during the Depression, but the

population still rose some, checking in at just short of 68,000 after a 12.4 percent increase. More growth lay ahead over the next two decades for the city.

Music

It was the era of the big bands, and big bands required a big dance floor.

Now, Charleston had one.

The open-air dance floor in Kanawha City shared its name with one of the well-known big bands of the day, Glen Gray's Casa Loma Orchestra, which was booked to play the opening night. (Ironically, the band itself was named after another Casa Loma, a hotel in Toronto where it had played an eight-month engagement in 1929.)

The name, however, was appropriate for the new venue in and of itself. It translated as "Hill House," and the Casa Loma was indeed at the base of a hill on MacCorkle Avenue at Mission Hollow Road.

The $15,000 project was largely the work of LaBabe Corey, whose family owned Corey's Arcade Fruit Market in the downtown Arcade on Virginia Street.

The 7,000-foot dance floor could accommodate as many as 1,000 people at a time. It wasn't the safest by modern standards: It was constructed of "an asbestos board that is particularly resilient and adaptable to dancing." Tables and folding chairs would be arrayed around it, with the bowl- or cave-style bandstand at one end. A removeable roof was also in the plans for fall and winter.

According a *The Charleston Gazette*, several nationally known orchestras were scheduled to play there, with Gene Krupa and His Orchestra booked during the opening week. Tommy Dorsey's orchestra would play the Casa Loma on April 28, 1941, and Woody

Herman would also make a stop there. (Tickets were 75 cents.)

In a case of "the show must go on," trumpeter Charlie Spivak played the venue during its first year right after surviving a crash en route. Several members of his band, however, didn't make it, so he recruited some local talent to fill in.

Speaking of local talent, West Virginia native Lloyd Neely brought his orchestra to the Casa Loma and played a nightly engagement there for a time, too. Neely's band, described in at least one press account as "one of the foremost bands in the country," also played student dances at Marshall College as well as at the Kanawha and Edgewood country clubs in Charleston.

Another act that played at Casa Loma had dancers seeing double. The Beverly Twins Orchestra, which served as the opening act for big bands like Tommy and Jimmy Dorsey, featured seven sets of identical twins. Some of them even swapped instruments during the show. They played at Casa Loma in 1941, but the band's rise was sidetracked by World War II, with seven of the 14 members joining the armed forces.

The band didn't regroup after the war, with cofounder Gene Beverly going on to become a booking agent instead.

Unfortunately, the situation was the same for other big bands, as well, which made things difficult at Casa Loma. With fewer bands coming to play in 1948, the venue purchased a new jukebox that it situated on the bandstand when live music wasn't available. The Wurlitzer 800 played a variety of selections, and you could dance to your heart's content on Wednesdays and Thursdays with no cover charge.

By the beginning of 1952, however, the lack of live music proved too much to overcome. Jukeboxes were available in other places, too, and with big bands out of vogue, the Casa Loma just wasn't as much of an attraction anymore, so the owners decided to tear it down.

The lumber would be used to build new homes on Tyler Mountain. A McDonald's restaurant later went up on the site.

1941

Cinema

The Village Theatre opened to serve residents of the Kanawha City neighborhood. The 500-seat theater opened in April with a showing of Bing Crosby, Mary Martin, and Basil Rathbone in the musical comedy *Rhythm on the River*.

The theater closed in 1988 and was later converted into office space. ...

The West Theatre building today. *Author photo*

The West Theatre opened at 1511 Washington St. that same year, in a building with a distinctive Art Deco façade that also included an eight-lane bowling alley called the West Bowling Center.

The $50,000, air-conditioned theater was originally going to be called the Sunset, and was decorated with a setting sun on the stage to give the impression of a sunset on an autumn day. The problem was, there already was a Sunset Theatre in town, just a short walk up the street.

The Sunset name was scrapped, and the West moniker was adopted instead.

With 1,000 seats, including a balcony, the theater also included "deeply upholstered chairs" and "love seats" at the end of each aisle, not to mention "carpet soft enough to sleep on." There was even a glass-enclosed nursery so moms could watch the show while their kids played.

Shows playing at the grand opening were *Flowing Gold* with John Garfield and *If I Had My Way* with Bing Crosby.

1942

Baseball

The Charleston Senators won the regular-season title in the Mid-Atlantic League with a 75-51 record, edging out the Dayton Ducks by a game and a half. Unfortunately for the Senators, they went cold in the playoff semifinals, where they were swept in three games by the Canton Terriers.

They didn't get a chance at redemption, either, because the league folded after that season.

Education

Morris Harvey College ended its Methodist affiliation, becoming an independent school.

Roller Skating

Dick and Margaret Barlow bought the failed ice rink at the Kanawha City bridge and converted into Barlow's Roller Rink.

Instead of phonograph records, they provided live music courtesy of organist Dorothy Musselman.

Three or four years later, they moved to a new location at 710 Virginia St. West, where 6,400 wheels on 800 pairs of skates could share the glass-like floor. The new facility was proclaimed the largest of its kind in the state at 205 by 60 feet, with an exterior lean-to of 15 feet running the length of the structure.

The Barlows weren't done yet, though.

In 1951, they completely remodeled their rink at a cost of $10,000, installing a new plastic floor.

At some point, the couple divorced, and Margaret Barlow remarried a firefighter named John Tucker. Margaret kept the skating rink but not her ex-husband's name, so it was natural that the rink got a new name: Skateland.

BARLOW'S SKATING RINK

Will Re-Open Tonight at 7:30

● **Completely Remodeled** ●
(at a cost of over $10,000)

● **NEW PLASTIC FLOOR**
EVERYTHING NEW

SKATING	
7:30 P.M. 'Til 10:30 P.M.	**50c**
MATINEE SAT. & SUN.	
1:30 P.M 'Til 4:00 P M	**35c**

710 VIRGINIA ST. W., 2-7635

You didn't want to tangle with Margaret, whatever name she went under. She was a fighter, bringing a number of lawsuits over the years, and running for a city council seat in 1967. She was known for packing heat, too. She carried a .38 revolver with her which, on one occasion, she used to hold a pair of thieves at bay until police arrived when she found them trying to strip her son's car.

During the civil rights era, however, Margaret Tucker would find herself on the wrong side of the fight over racial segregation. Ultimately, it would cost her the skating rink.

1943

Radio

WCHS won a Peabody Award (presented annually by the National Association of Broadcasters for radio excellence) for a show titled *The Home Front*.

The program, narrated by Bert Sonis, encouraged wives of service members to call in if they were having problems getting their military allotment checks. The station would then provide them with assistance resolving those problems.

Two years later, station director Howard Chernoff traveled to Europe as a war correspondent for the West Virginia Network, an independent radio network. Chernoff interviewed service members from West Virginia, then sent the tapes to CBS in New York, which broadcast them. He also occasionally broadcast live.

1944

Football

Portsmouth High appeared to have its game against Charleston High won. But then Charlie Coleman gathered in a kickoff at the 3-yard line in the waning seconds and ran it back 97 yards for a touchdown and a 20-19 victory in what was described three decades later as "the most thrilling finish any football game ever had at old Laidley Field."

1945

Fast Food

The name Mandt was all but synonymous with hot dogs and root beer down the road in Huntington for years, where the

Mandt family ran Stewart's Original Drive-In.

In the Spring Hill neighborhood of South Charleston, a different Mandt made a different restaurant an institution. Charlie Mandt had started serving up hot dogs at Fred's Park, named for his father, Fred Mandt, on Charleston's west side seven years earlier in 1938.

Looking back on his career in a 1976 interview with *The Daily Mail*, Charlie said, "Thirty-eight is a magic number for me. Started in '38, got married in '38, and the business has been good to me for 38 years."

Charlie opened up his own place in Spring Hill in 1945 when, he said, "there was nothing down here beside me except space, and a big cornfield out back between here and the river." There was a service station across the street, alongside the Spring Hill post office.

Hot dogs and root beer were the biggest attractions, but milkshakes were popular, too. On some days, he served 150 of them. The 28-ounce shakes were so thick you had to eat them with a spoon, and they were all made by hand. You could get one for a dime.

Or you could just pull up beside the curb, and one of five serving girls would run out to sell you a hot dog. The dogs were a dime, just like the milkshakes, and the root beer was a nickel.

Mandt's Drive-In stayed open for 38 years before finally closing in 1976.

Football

South Charleston High won the state championship nod in the next-to-last year the title was awarded by the Sportswriters Association.

1947

The Trail Drive-In opened with a massive screen as the first outdoor theater in the area. *Jay Harvey, Cinema Treasures, Creative Commons 2.0*

Cinema

The Trail Drive-In brought outdoor movies to the Charleston area, but you had to drive a few miles south of town to get there. Located on U.S. 60 in Belle, the Trail had a screen that looked like a castle or fortress.

"The Trail Drive-In Outdoor Theatre will bring to the public many advantages," read an ad for the August 1 grand opening.

It declared that the new venue would benefit everyone from mothers with small children, to "stout people who find the average theatre chairs uncomfortable," not to mention the elderly and people in poor health. "And to those who are hard of hearing, the Trail Drive-In's individually controlled speaker for each car affords them pleasures in sound pictures heretofore unfound."

The Trail debuted with a screening of *Do You Love Me*, a musical featuring Maureen O'Hara opposite bandleader Harry James (who played a bandleader, naturally). A musical cartoon called *Choo Choo Amigo* was also on the bill, with shows scheduled for 8 and 10 p.m.

But the big attraction was the theater itself. The $100,000 venue had room for 650 cars and a screen that measured 50 by 70 feet. E.R. Custer, who owned the company that built it, declared it to be the "largest of its kind in the U.S."

Still, there was more to the screen than just a screen. At its base was an actual motel with three or four rooms, along with a snack bar that was open on the screen side at night. But it also had service windows facing the street that allowed it to remain open during daylight hours, as well.

"No expense has been spared to obtain the very best in equipment for comfortable rest rooms, modern refreshment stand and spacious grounds complete with picnic facilities," the opening-day ad declared.

The builder wasn't finished in the area, either. A year later, in the summer of 1948, Custer and his partners opened the Valley Drive-In in St. Albans. The Belle was demolished in 1977 to make room for a lumber store. The Valley Drive-In closed 19 years later, but the screen remained standing. It, too, became the site of a lumber business.

Dining

Alex Schoenbaum grew up in Huntington, but he first made his mark as a businessman in Charleston.

That was after he made his mark on the football field.

For a while, it looked like Schoenbaum would be best remembered for his exploits on the gridiron. As a standout tackle for Ohio State, he twice was named honorable mention All-American and was picked 55th overall in the NFL Draft by the Brooklyn Dodgers football team.

But instead of a career in pro football, Schoenbaum headed back to West Virginia — Charleston, to be specific. Before he'd gone off to college, he had spent time as a pin boy at his father's Arcade Recreation bowling alley and pool hall in Huntington. (This was in the days before automated pinsetters, so youngsters at the end of each lane would reset the pins by hand after every shot.) But his family owned a bowling center in Charleston, too, so when he finished college, he went there to manage the place.

You don't have to be an
Eskimo
to enjoy the
GOOD FOOD at the
PARKETTE

• CHILLI
• HOT DOGS
• HAMBURGERS
• BANQUET-BURGERS
• BAR-B-QUES
• CHICKEN
• SEAFOOD

For in all kinds of weather you still get the same good food and courteous service that go to make the PARKETTE one of CHARLESTON'S finest eating places.

THE **Parkette**
"ON THE BOULEVARD"

Then, in 1947, he decided to on a different project: He opened a restaurant next to the bowling alley, which he dubbed the Parkette Drive-In.

An ad in the *Charleston Daily Mail* during the winter of 1951 declared that you didn't "have to be an Eskimo to enjoy the good food at the Parkette. For in all kinds of weather, you still get the same courteous service that go to make the Parkette one of Charleston's finest eating places."

The Parkette "on the Boulevard" — Kanawha Boulevard West

at Patrick Street — offered a selection of dishes such as hot dogs, chili, burgers, barbecue sandwiches, seafood, and chicken.

In 1952, Parkette became the Big Boy licensee for West Virginia and expanded from there: An ad in the February *Daily Mail* boasted, "You can now get a Big Boy at the Parkette. Don't miss this sensational treat!" (The affiliation, which began in 1952, would end about three decades later.) Big Boy had started out at Bob's on the West Coast, but Schoenbaum was owned the East. He would go on to open so many new restaurants that his chain would eventually become the biggest licensee in the region.

At first, though, it was strictly local.

After the first Parkette opened, others quickly followed. There was one at 172 Summers St., one on 36th Street in Kanawha City, and one on Third Avenue in South Charleston.

You could get fried chicken with fries or potato salad, coleslaw, and a buttered roll for a dollar; a "Poor Boy's Meal" for 70 cents that included a Big Boy, fries, coleslaw, lettuce and tomato; or a King Fish sandwich for 45 cents. You could even order a pizza by calling the Parkette "Pizza House."

The Parkette name remained after the licensing agreement with Big Boy was signed, but it became known as Parkette Big Boy Shoppes.

Still, Schoenbaum wanted something catchier. "Parkette" wasn't exactly original. There was a Parkette Drive-In in Lexington, for example, and more to the point, there was a chain of Parkettes under entirely different ownership in Huntington, where Schoenbaum had grown up. (In fact, Schoenbaum would open two restaurants there before too long, in 1956.)

The question was what the new name should be.

To decide, Schoenbaum elicited help from the public: He invited everyone to submit ideas for the new name and offered plenty of incentive for doing so. Those submitting suggestions didn't even need to buy a Big Boy.

The grand prize would be a 1954 Lincoln Capri Hardtop Convertible, and 25 runner-up prizes were to be awarded as well. They included a new 24-inch television, a Tappan range, and an Admiral refrigerator, along with a dozen table radios and eight $25 savings bonds.

The winners were chosen by an ad agency in Columbus, Ohio. An insurance rep from Charleston named Paul S. Edens won the car... and promptly sold it.

"As you probably know, it was a very difficult project to pick a winner from the thousands of entries we received," Schoenbaum wrote. "We trust you are as please with our choice as we are, and that, 'let's go down to Shoney's' will become a regular part of your vocabulary."

It appears to have gone over well, because by 1998, Shoney's had grown into a chain of more than 1,300 restaurants in 34 states.

There was even a motel chain that operated for some years beginning in 1975 called Shoney's Inn.

Shoney's would be immortalized in a song by country artist Joe Diffie called "Third Rock from the Sun," in which a truck "hits a Big Boy in the Shoney's parking lot," triggering a chain of events in which the Big Boy statue hits a bank clock, which in turn strikes a light pole that causes a power outage all over the city.

And rumors that a giant alien had landed at the mall.

No word on whether any of this fictional account was supposed to have occurred in Charleston, but anything's possible. The original Parkette/Shoney's on Charleston's West Side closed in December of 1975.

Education

Morris Harvey College moved to its current location on the south bank of the Kanawha River. Hundreds of people gathered to watch the school's buildings ferried across the river.

The campus at this point consisted of five government surplus buildings, a Quonset hut, three barracks-style buildings, a cafeteria/assembly hall, and a small frame building.

Another building, Riggleman Hall, would be added in 1951.

1948

The Stone & Thomas Building today. *Author photo*

Retail

Stone & Thomas was to West Virginia what Bullock's was to Los Angeles and Rich's was to Atlanta. It was a retail institution.

It had started off in Wheeling back in the mid-19th century and had acquired a stake in The People's Store, a major clothing retailer in Charleston dating back to the early years of the century, during the 1930s.

Now, in 1948, it was opening a new store described as "the most modern in the country." Even today, driving by the building, it lives up to that description. Although it's vacant now, the Streamline Moderne design still stands out.

At the time, there was so much excitement around the November grand opening that 15,000 people showed up for the two-hour ceremony, blocking traffic as they waited to enter what *The Charleston Gazette* described as a store "different from any department store in West Virginia."

Track and Field

Stonewall Jackson High began a string of eight consecutive years as state track and field champion, the longest such uninterrupted streak in state history.

1949

Baseball

Charleston had been without a baseball team since 1942, but that was about to change.

The transformation began with a new stadium: Watt Powell Park, built in 1948 and named for the man who epitomized baseball in the city.

Watt Powell had never been a great ballplayer. He'd played parts of two seasons with San Francisco in the Pacific Coast League, but he'd spent most of his 12 seasons tooling around the low minor leagues in places like Danville and Roanoke, Virginia, before ending his pro career on the field as player-manager at Charleston in 1916.

He stayed in Charleston (where he also managed a pool hall

at the Kanawha Hotel) to play for and manage the Senators semipro team after that and in 1931, was instrumental in bringing the team back into the pro ranks as president of the ballclub when it joined the Middle Atlantic League.

Powell's teams had played at Kanawha Park, but a new field was needed for a new version of the Senators, so a $350,000 bond was passed to build a new park on the site of the old one. Measuring 327 and 325 feet down the foul lines and 380 to straightaway center field, it had room for 5,500 fans and became home to the new Charleston Senators in the Class A Central League.

The league had begun play with a dozen teams in 1948, but had lost more than half its members; Charleston's entry brought the membership back up to six.

Fans were so enthusiastic about the new team and the new ballpark that they turned out in droves, as the Senators easily topped the league in attendance and averaged more fans per game (2,716) than during any other season in Charleston history.

The team itself finished in fourth place, barely qualifying for the four-team playoff with a record of 67-68, but the Senators shocked the first-place Dayton Indians 3 games to 1 in the first round of the playoffs to earn a spot in the finals, where they fell to the Grand Rapids Jets 4 games to 2.

The Senators stayed in the Central League for the next two seasons, leading the circuit in attendance both years, before the league folded.

Lodging

The ad in the Sunday newspaper was a sure tip-off: You didn't go to the El Rancho Inn for a restful night, at least not first and foremost.

The ad declared the El Rancho to be "The Party Place."

That made sense, considering motels didn't usually advertise for patrons in their hometown paper. But locals (at least a certain segment of them) loved to party, and they went to the El Rancho to do it.

The El Rancho opened its doors in 1949, adopting a western motif. It wasn't exactly an original name: There were dozens and perhaps hundreds of El Ranchos across the country, many of them scattered in the desert Southwest. That's probably one reason the one on U.S. 60 west of Charleston made a point of saying it didn't belong to a chain.

Originally just a motel, offering "A Little of the West back East," El Rancho added a restaurant in 1952, which became an entertainment hub thanks to in part to Dick Reid, who owned the establishment with his wife, Irene. A local disc jockey and television host for WKNA and later WCHS, Dick Reid broadcast shows live from the site.

Business was so good the motel expanded in 1957 and the restaurant's seating capacity was boosted to 325 six years later. Three separate new dining areas were added — the Frontier, Thunderbird, and Patio — to accommodate large groups.

The El Rancho in St. Albans. *Author collection*

STEPHEN H. PROVOST

Shifting Signals

1950–1959

The arch at Charleston High School was preserved after the school itself closed and can now be seen at Capital High School. *Author photo*

1950

Milestones

Charleston's population grew to 73,501 after an 8.2 percent increase in the 1940s.

Weather

Thanksgiving was on November 23 in 1950, so winter was still almost a month away. But you wouldn't have known it if you'd gotten out of bed the following day in Charleston or just about anywhere else in West Virginia.

That's when a frigid storm of epic proportions came barreling across the Mountain State, dropping an unprecedented 25.6 inches of snow on Charleston on over the next two days. It was a record for a single storm.

And the weather wasn't done yet.

On November 27, it was (fittingly) 27 degrees, and more snow was falling in Charleston. At Coburn Creek, 63.2 inches fell in a seven-day period starting on Thanksgiving, and at Pickens, 67.5 inches fell. Those figures still stood as of 2018 as the highest totals ever for West Virginia.

The weeklong fiasco cut off half the cities in the state and collapsed the roof on West Virginia University's new recreation center. Schools were closed, and Christmas shopping was nonexistent as people stayed inside. Snow drifts as much as 8 feet high were reported. Mail service was interrupted, and phone lines were overtaxed by callers trying to make sure family members were safe. Stranded Thanksgiving travelers piled onto trains because the buses weren't running.

The snowstorm became known as the Great Appalachian Storm of 1950, and the United Press called it the worst snowstorm in November history.

1951

Basketball

The Charleston High boys hadn't made it to the finals in 18 years, but they got there in '51 on the shoulders of one "Hot Rod" Hundley.

Just a sophomore, the 6-foot-4 phenom averaged 22.4 points a game as the team compiled a record of 21-6. But the even he couldn't get the Cougars past their final obstacle: Woodrow Wilson, which tamed them in the finals 62-54 to win the first of four consecutive Class A titles.

Charleston would get its rematch with Woodrow Wilson in the 1957 finals, after Hundley had moved on to West Virginia University, but the result would be the same, with Wilson prevailing over a 25-3 Charleston High team 82-70.

"Hot" Rod Hundley went on to star with the Las Angeles Lakers, but in 1951, the sophomore led Charleston High School's basketball team to the state finals.

Hundley, meanwhile, played two more years at Charleston, but the Cougars never managed to get back to the finals despite posting records of 19-5 during his junior year and 22-3 when he was a senior. Hundley's scoring average increased each year, to 25.4 points a game in 1952 and 33.7 the following year.

He finished his career averaging 27.1 points in 45 games with a career total of 1,956 points, a Kanawha Valley Conference record that still held up two decades later.

Trivillian's at the base of the bridge in Kanawha City was one of two pharmacies operated by Nick Trivillian. *Author photo*

Retail

Trivillian's Pharmacy had everything you needed for your medicinal and personal care needs at two locations: on Quarrier Street downtown and at the foot of the bridge in Kanawha City. Bonus at the second location, which had opened just a year earlier: Plenty of free parking.

The pharmacy's February sale items included a 4-ounce size of Boric acid for just 11 cents (regular 20 cents), tincture of green soap for 19 cents, and mercurochrome in an applicator bottle for 12 cents.

Other deals would get you a 20-ounce bottle of Lavoris mouthwash for 79 cents, Halo shampoo or Noxzema skin cream for 29 cents, Dr. Lyon's tooth powder for 39 cents, and Benex shave cream for 49 cents.

Camp Drug at Five Corners and Lowman's on Washington Street were two other neighborhood pharmacies. *Author photos*

Other neighborhoods had their own drugstores. Lowman's out on Washington Street opened in 1927. And Camp Drug offered its West Side customers fresh strawberry, banana, black walnut, or pistachio ice cream at Five Corners in 1931.

Trivillian's dated all the way back to 1896, when Fred Klostermeyer opened it under his name. He hired Nick Trivillian to work the soda fountain and do some stocking at the pharmacy, and Trivillian did such a good job that Klostermeyer offered him the business at the end of the Depression on the condition that he assume its debts.

Trivillian accepted, and the pharmacy became his.

1952

Baseball

Charleston kept moving up in the baseball world.

A little more than a year after the Central League's demise, yet another version of the Senators emerged, this time in the AAA American Association, when the Toledo Mud Hens moved to Charleston midway through the season.

The ballclub finished last in the eight-team circuit with a 46-107 record.

They would finish in the cellar the next three seasons, too, before moving up to sixth place in 1956.

It was a slow climb.

1953

Aviation

Chuck Yeager, the pilot who broke the sound barrier in 1947, was known for his speed.

West Virginians had never seen a jet plane in action before. So Yeager — who was a native of Myra, West Virginia, about an hour to the west — decided to give them a treat. If they blinked, though, they might have missed it.

Yeager's plane took off from the Kanawha Airport and streaked toward the Capitol dome. Then, suddenly, he dove toward the river and followed its course no more than 50 feet above the water, doing 600 miles an hour.

Almost before anyone knew what was happening, he was approaching the South Side Bridge. But instead of pulling up to fly over it, he stayed on course and dipped *underneath* it.

Chuck Yeager, the man who broke the sound barrier, once flew *under* the South Side Bridge.

He then made a 45-degree turn and sped off to California.

The bridge was later named in his honor.

So was the airport where he took off on his daredevil bridge-diving journey. Kanawha Airport, opened in 1947, became Yeager Airport in 1985.

Cinema

Fred Helwig opened the Owens Drive-In, with a single screen and enough room for 450 cars, at 6231 MacCorkle Ave. SE. It would be moved in to nearby Marmet, where viewers could enjoy electric car heaters — in order to make way for a new Kmart, which was built in 1972.

The theater stayed in its new location until 1985, opening for a flea market from 9 a.m. to 5 p.m. Sundays (admission was 50 cents a car). It was ultimately torn down and replaced by a Kroger and Hardee's.

Crime

When a prominent person is murdered, it usually doesn't go unsolved — especially if the victim is the publisher of the city's newspaper.

But that's exactly what happened in the puzzling case of Juliet Staunton Clark, publisher of the *Charleston Daily Mail*. She was also president of the Charleston Garden Club and Junior League, not to mention the widow of Alaska's former territorial governor. Her grandfather on her mother's side had been the first mayor of Huntington.

And Clark herself was prominent in local Republican politics.

But somehow, none of that mattered when it came to solving the case. Clark had been running the newspaper for three years, since her husband's death of a heart attack in 1950. She was, apparently, popular with the staff; she didn't micromanage them, and she'd occasionally drop food off at the office for her employees.

She was 59 years old on the night of August 21, the last time anyone saw her alive.

Both her son, Lyell Clay, and son-in-law Arch Alexander Jr. visited her that evening, with Alexander leaving the house around 9 p.m. He'd come to the house to visit his 3-year-old son, who was staying with his grandmother while his mother (Juliet's daughter) was in the hospital.

Juliet was still awake at 10:30, when she ended a phone call with another woman, and a neighbor heard Clark's raised voice about a half-hour later from across the way. She brushed it off, though, thinking Clark was simply saying goodnight to someone. It was the last time anyone heard Clark's voice.

The house lights stayed on overnight, and were still on when her maid arrived the next morning. The door was ajar, too. She didn't think much of it, but when she entered the house, she was puzzled to find the kitchen clean, knowing that it was her employer's habit to make breakfast for herself each morning.

But it was when she got to the living room that she faced a truly shocking and disturbing scene: Juliet Staunton Clark, a woman without any known enemies, was lying face-down on the living room floor. Her skull had been bashed in so badly that investigators thought at first she had been shot. But they later realized she'd been brutally attacked by a blunt object.

Fortunately, the young boy, Archie, was found safe in his room. (Sadly, he would die not long afterward of burns he sustained in an accident.)

A sliver of wood, believed to have been from the murder weapon, was found nearby, but the weapon itself was never recovered even though divers combed the Kanawha River in search of it.

Indeed, the case offered few clues. Clark's valuables, including an expensive ring and watch she wore, hadn't been taken, and all that was missing was a red billfold that — like the murder weapon — was never recovered. The tips that came pouring in to the police department didn't help much, either. And a lot of tips came in because the public had plenty of incentive to offer them.

The newspaper immediately offered a $2,500 reward for information leading to the arrest and conviction of the killer. Early the following year, it was raised to $15,000, and as late as 1959, a reward for $1,000 was still being offered. But there was never enough evidence, in the eyes of authorities, to press charges — even though Mayor John Copenhaver said there wasn't much doubt in his mind who had killed Clark.

Copenhaver said the police "perhaps" knew who committed the crime, but that "knowing and proving are two different things."

What led Copenhaver to those conclusions? He never said.

But considering robbery was an unlikely motive for the killing, there must have been another reason. What was it? The answer was never found, but statistics show that women are most often killed by family members or intimate partners: In 2007, for example 64 percent of female homicides fell into this category, according to the U.S. Department of Justice.

Furthermore, it is worth noting that polygraph expert Dr. Fred Inbau had conducted lie-detector tests on 20 people in 1953. Among them was Arch Alexander, who claimed he had nothing to hide.

The results of that test were kept hidden over the years until early 2021, when the results were uncovered in documents left in Copenhaver's bottom desk drawer on his death in 1959. They came to light when the person in their possession shared them with *Charleston Gazette-Mail* reporter Rick Steelhammer more than six decades later.

Inbau's report concluded that Alexander wasn't telling the truth when he denied involvement in Clark's murder. But he qualified that statement by saying there was a "remote possibility" that Alexander was telling the truth. Meanwhile, polygraph exams administered to Clark's sons Lyell (who was there that evening) and Buck Clay both "indicated their innocence of any involvement in the Clark murder."

Since polygraph tests are rarely admissible in court, the presence of the results in Copenhaver's desk would provide a plausible explanation why the mayor said he believed he knew the killer's identity, but that there wasn't enough evidence to prove it.

Arch Alexander, a lawyer, never addressed the subject of his mother-in-law's killing in the years that followed, and no new evidence surfaced that warranted bringing charges. No one was arrested, and the case remained open and unsolved.

Television

WKNA was in the wrong place at the right time.

The new TV station got there first, hitting the Charleston market in 1953 with that most exciting of television extravaganzas, the test pattern.

But lack of excitement wasn't the main problem — the programming would come soon enough. Lack of signal was. WKNA was broadcasting on the UHF frequency at Channel 49. That created two issues: reception and access.

Reception was a problem because of the hilly terrain around Charleston blocked UHF signals or made them come in "snowy" if you were just a few miles away. The station's film and promotion director, Ted McKay, lived just 12 miles away. But he had to rig up an antenna on a mast 20 feet high to get a snowy picture at home, which only lasted until the trees' leaves came back in spring. Then, he got nothing.

The second problem was more basic: access. McKay had a TV that could receive UHF signals, but many residents didn't. So even if they lived right in Charleston, they could only get stations with a VHF frequency. Customers could either buy a set that with UHF access or spend $70 less for one without it. Guess which one they chose.

WKNA tried a marketing campaign that urged viewers, "Don't buy half a TV set," but it had little effect. And advertisers shied away from the station because of its limited penetration.

Compounding the problem: The station was affiliated with the DuMont and ABC networks, but WSAZ in Huntington had the same affiliations — while also carrying shows from NBC and CBS. Because it was operating on VHF, Charleston viewers could see programs from Huntington more easily than they could from their local station, plus they had a bigger selection of shows.

WKNA tried to lure viewers by touting its exclusive

programming, such as *Liberace* and *Drew Person Reports*, but to no avail.

The situation was bad enough when WKNA was the only station in town, but it became even more problematic a year later, when WCHS signed on as Charleston's first VHF station down at Channel 8.

WKNA had brought several employees over from its radio station (with the same call letters), including McKay, program director Don Hays, manager George Gray, and on-air hosts Dick Reid and Ed Miller. Reid joined Sarah Harshbarger to present *What's Cookin'*, a daily cooking show, and he also teamed up with McKay on *TV Juke Box*.

Reid also developed a show for kids called *The 49ers Club* and had another show called the *Lucky 8 Ranch*, but he jumped ship for a better gig the following year at WCHS.

With a tiny budget constrained by limited ad revenues, WKNA staged a newscast without any footage to complement the camera's view of newscaster Bill Barrett sitting behind a desk. The weather map was just a board that was wiped down at the end of each day.

The station showed programming with titles such as *Captain Video, Music Mountain Style, Strike It Rich, Virginia's Home Journal,* and *On Your Account.* It also aired soap operas such as *Search for Tomorrow*, the religious-themed *The Brighter Day, Love of Life*, and *The Secret Storm.*

Another early soap, *The Seeking Heart*, found a place in the lineup, too. Daytime serials were generally just 15 minutes in those days, and this CBS offering involved romantic tension between a married doctor and his assistant. The show only lasted one season, just slightly longer than WKNA was on the air.

The station announced it was suspending its operation on Feb. 12, 1955 in order to "re-evaluate the potential successful operation of a UHF station in the Charleston market," according to a statement by owner Joe L. Smith Jr. "WKNA-TV in the very near future hopes to announce a resumption date."

It never did.

Barrett, the news anchor, went to work for United Press covering the statehouse and worked his way up to assistant managing editor in Washington, D.C., in 1975.

Dick Reid, meanwhile, continued with WCHS for some time, hosting a show called *Record Hop* through the 1950s and becoming known locally as the "dean of rock 'n' roll." He also hosted live Record Hop events.

Sadly, both Reid and Barrett died young: Reid after a three-week hospitalization in 1966 at the age of 44, and Barrett in 1977 at age 55.

Reid was inducted into the West Virginia Broadcasting Hall of Fame in 2007.

1954

Auto Racing

Skyline Raceway was open opposite Daniel Boone State Park on Piedmont Road, aka U.S. 60.

According to a press report, the raceway was "so elevated that a rain of several hours duration, should it subside just one hour before race time, will not interfere with racing."

The new track staged a 50-lap championship trophy race on Halloween featuring 50 or more top stock car racers from West Virginia, Ohio, Kentucky, and Virginia.

Cinema

The Frontier Drive In announced its grand opening a week before Independence Day with a double feature of John Wayne in

Hondo and a short film called *Black Fury* about tracking a rogue bear in the Georgia and Florida swamps. Admission was 60 cents and free to children younger than 12, who could enjoy a color cartoon as part of the bill.

There was a snack bar on site, but if you wanted something different, you could head to the 21 Stopette Drive In or Duncan's Drive-In, both of which were right on Sissonville Road on the way to the Frontier. You could buy a cold beer at either place, and you could also get hot dogs, burgers, sandwiches, shakes, and salads at Duncan's.

CHILDREN WILL LIKE

LUCKY 8 RANCH

AND GROWN UPS WILL TOO!
WITH BOSSMAN DICK REID
5:00-6:00 P.M. MONDAY thru FRIDAY

SEE THESE FINE PROGRAMS SOON ON CHANNEL 8

ANNIE OAKLEY
6:00—Tuesday

RANGE RIDER
6:00—Wednesday

BARKER BILL
6:15—Thursday

CBS

SUPERMAN
6:15—Thursday

CISCO KID
6:00—Friday

BADGE AND BULLETS
1:30—4:30 p. m., Saturday

on WCHS-TV Channel 8
316,000 WATTS

CBS   THERE IS NO TV STATION IN THE UNITED STATES   DUMONT
MORE POWERFUL THAN WCHS-TV, CHANNEL 8

Television

WCHS debuted as Charleston's first VHF television station on August 15, 1954, broadcasting with the aid of a 949-foot tower on Nease Mountain off Route 35.

A newspaper account declared that the "gigantic tower" was "one of the tallest man-made structures in the state," operating on 316,000 watts of power: "West Virginia's newest television station is now beaming its signal to an estimated two million viewers."

The station, checking in at Channel 8 on the dial, began as a CBS affiliate. It would switch to ABC in 1958 before going back to its original affiliation three or four years later.

Early lineups featured shows such as *My Favorite Husband*, *The Jackie Gleason Show*, *Disneyland*, *The Red Skelton Revue*, and *Ed Sullivan's Toast of the Town*.

Locally produced content included a cooking show called *Katie's Kitchen*, hosted by Katie Doonan in the late '50s. There was also *Uncle Willie's Popcorn Theater*, hosted by a character called Uncle Willie. He was played by George "Sleepy" Jeffers, who had come to Charleston from Shreveport, Louisiana, where he'd been known as "The Smiling Troubadour."

Jeffers also had a radio show on KTIP, but as Uncle Willie, he appeared as gap-toothed clownish character in suspenders, an oversized tie, wig and derby hat.

One of the station's mainstays was *Record Hop*, hosted by Dick Reid. The show began as a daily program in 1957 and became a weekly Saturday night offering the following year.

The format was a whole lot like American Bandstand. As described in *Billboard Music Week*, the show featured "teen-agers dancing on camera and guest shots — live or taped — by visiting record artists."

"The dancers, tagged 'The Record Hoppers,' are recruited, trained and directed by Jim Lucas, who operates a local ballroom dancing school."

The show kept things interesting by adopting various themes, such as Halloween parties, New Year's Eve balls, proms, and a Father's Day week that featured parents and their kids. The show aired from the WCHS studio most of the year but switched to Rock Lake Pool during the summer.

Valley Bell Dairy and Henry's Men and Boys Shops were sponsors throughout its first three years on the air. Shoney's,

Cohen Drugs, Embees Ladieswear, Gilmar Records, and Rock Lake Pool also supported the show at various times.

It was still on the air as of March 1961, airing in the 6 to 7:30 p.m. timeslot.

1956

Basketball

Zeke from Cabin Creek put the tiny town of East Bank, population 1,068, on the map, along with East Bank High School. Until now, Cabin Creek had been known primarily for the rich oilfield that had made millions for Pure Oil. But from this point forward, it would be known as part of the nickname belonging to a basketball wizard named Jerry West.

East Bank was just about 20 miles from

Jerry West in 1959 at West Virginia.

Charleston and wouldn't have normally been any match for bigger schools like Charleston High, but Jerry West was the great equalizer. He paced the Pioneers to the state title in 1956, when they posted a 23-5 record and topped Morgantown (24-2) by a 71-58 count in the state finals.

West scored 39 points in the championship game, including

all of his team's 16 points in the second quarter as the Pioneers built a slim 31-29 lead before pulling away in the second half. He fouled out with just under 5½ minutes to play and received a standing ovation, finishing with a tournament record 56 rebounds.

Once East Bank had claimed the title, a sign appeared at the edge of town that paid tribute to their star player with the message "East Bank. Now West Bank."

West finished his two-year high school career with a 25.9-point scoring average, including a conference-record 34.9 points a game as a senior. His point total of 926 was a state record for the most in a single season.

"Mr. Clutch," as he was also known, would play 93 games during three seasons at WVU, averaging 24.8 points a game, and taking the Mountaineers to the NCAA finals in his senior season, when he was named the tournament's outstanding player even though West Virginia fell to California 71-70 in the championship game.

He was also co-captain of the 1960 gold medal Olympic team.

But the best was still to come.

Signing with the Los Angeles Lakers in 1960, he made a total of 14 All-Star teams and averaged 27 points per game in a playing career that lasted until 1974. He was the league's top scorer in 1970, a year after being named the NBA Finals MVP in 1969 even though the Lakers lost to the Boston Celtics.

The Celtics had the Lakers' number in the Finals throughout the sixties. But the Lakers finally broke through in 1972, winning the title with what was, at the time, the best record in NBA history. West was the All-Star Game MVP that year.

He later served as a coach before beginning a long career as an executive, winning eight NBA championships and twice being named the league's Executive of the Year. His silhouette was even used as the model for the NBA's iconic logo.

1957

Retail

A store called Tall Fashions was opening in Charleston at Hale and Quarrier, advertising itself as "the only shop in West Virginia devoted exclusively to fashions for the girl 5'7" or over."

Its motto?

"Always the height of style."

1958

Baseball

If you win just one state title in your school's history, you might as well make it memorable, and Stonewall Jackson did just that.

The Generals had never won a state baseball crown before 1958, and they never won another after that, but The Wall's day in the sun was as brilliant as any could get. They rapped out 20 hits against Gary in a seven-inning game that was as miserable for their opponents as it was memorable for them.

Gary fielders committed 11 errors, leading to nine unearned Stonewall runs. Seven of those errors (including four by the shortstop) came in the first inning alone, when the Generals scored eight runs. They never looked back from there, crossing the plate 13 more times in a 21-1 blowout.

As of 2021, it was still the most runs ever scored in a West Virginia state championship baseball game. ...

Charleston fans had waited a long time for a successful team in the American Association, and they finally had one. After several consecutive losing seasons, the Senators topped the standings with a record of 89-62, a healthy 7½ games better than the second-place Wichita Braves.

Pitcher Jim Davie (17-5) ranked second in the league in both wins and earned-run average (2.45). He would play 11 games with the Tigers the following season. In fact, more than 30 players on the Senators' 1958 roster played in the majors at one time or another.

But the Senators' regular-season supremacy failed to translate into postseason success: They lost to the fourth-place Denver Bears 4 games to 3 in the playoffs.

Nineteen-sixty would be the last season for the Senators in Charleston.

The *Charleston Gazette-Mail* building in 2021. *Author photo*

Journalism

The Charleston Daily Mail and *Charleston Gazette* signed a joint operating agreement to merge production and distribution operations, although their editorial staffs remained fully separate. They also began producing the *Sunday Gazette-Mail*, using both their staffs.

That arrangement would remain in place until 1991, when the *Gazette* staff alone assume responsibility for the Sunday content. In 2015, the two newspapers would merge entirely into a new publication called the *Gazette-Mail*.

Recreation

The Putt-Putt Miniature Golf Course opened next to the Owens Drive-In in the Kanawha City neighborhood. A special guest was on hand to mark the occasion: Miss Joan Honeycutt, winner of the Putt-Putt Search for Beauty Contest.

The honor came with a $500 award.

1959

Basketball

South Charleston capped a 24-3 season with a 73-67 win over Fairmont to claim its first state boys' basketball title.

Tickets for the "Vacation Dance Party" were on sale at Gorby's in South Charleston, seen here. *Author photo*

Music

The rock concert was just starting to evolve and was nothing like it is today. Promoters would put together a slate of acts with recent hits for marathon rock shows and dances.

One such show, billed as a "Vacation Dance Party," came to the Charleston Civic Center on June 24.

The four-hour show featured seven different acts, all appearing in person and promoting their latest singles: Freddy Cannon ("Tallahassee Lassie"), Frankie Ford ("Sea Cruise"), Johnny and the Hurricanes ("Crossfire"), The Mystics ("Hush-a-Bye"), Gary Stites ("Lonely for You") and Carl Dobkins Jr. ("My Heart's an Open Book").

You could see all these performers for just $1.25 in advance, with tickets available at Gorby's in South Charleston, Bill's Card Shop in the Gateway Shopping Center, Music Box in Kanawha City, and other outlets. Or you could wait and pay 50 cents more at the box office.

Retail

Heck's was the name of the store, but there was no one actually named Heck. Downtown Charleston's newest store opened at the tail end of the 1950s in an empty building that had previously been a Kaiser-Fraser auto showroom.

"Heck's" was actually a mashup of the three owners' names: Fred Haddad contributed the "H," brothers Tom and Lester Ellis shared the "E," and Douglas Cook got two letters: the "C" and the "K." Haddad and the Ellis brothers were former rivals at stores in Madison, West Virginia, while Cook was working for a wholesaler.

Haddad served as chairman and board president, while Cook handled advertising and merchandising. The partners invested $35,000 in the new enterprise. It would soon be worth far more than that.

In fact, the Charleston store went over so well, they opened a much bigger store on U.S. 60 between Charleston and St. Albans in 1961, and another just a couple of weeks after that in Huntington.

The U.S. 60 store, which carried a price tag of $500,000, called for 35,000 feet of floor space, making it the state's largest one-story retail site at the time. That was about three times the size of the flagship downtown store. It would be air-conditioned with tile floors, an acoustic ceiling, and four automatic doors.

A sign from the Heck's chain, which started in an old automobile dealership in downtown Charleston and expanded to become a $300 million business.

Like other stores in the fast-growing discount sector, it would have cash registers (eight of them) at the front, rather than in different departments, as was typical for traditional department stores. There would be a snack bar, building supply and hardware department, tire center, and parking spaces for 300 cars.

The expansion continued from there: into Kentucky, Maryland, and Virginia by 1963. In 1966, Heck's dipped its toe in the water of the drugstore market, opening a location in South Charleston and another on Capitol Street.

By 1968, the chain had struck a deal to sell its 20 stores to the J.J. Newberry Discount Chain, but the deal fell through — which was a good thing, at least in the short term, because there was plenty more money to be made.

Haddad sold his stock and retired in 1983, at which point the company had posted 24 straight years of profits. Not long after he left, everything went south.

By the mid-1980s, the chain had 166 stores and more than 8,000 employees in nine states. It was worth more than $300 million. But the rise of Walmart and Kmart (which had stores two or three times as big) and hard economic times in West Virginia and elsewhere led to the chain's demise, and it filed for bankruptcy in 1987.

STEPHEN H. PROVOST

Rights & Rockets

1960–1969

1960

Boxing

When Tunney stepped into the ring, he was convinced he could beat the man standing in front of him, who was making his pro boxing debut.

This wasn't Gene Tunney, though, and the man he was facing wasn't any ordinary first-time fighter. Tunney Hunsaker was the police chief in Fayetteville, a small town about an hour down the road from Charleston. And the man he was facing off against was the Olympic light heavyweight champion: one Cassius Clay, later to be known as Muhammad Ali.

Hunsaker was, by this point in his career, the kind of opponent tailor-made for up-and-coming heavyweights: someone who would give the prospects ring experience without posing any real threat. He'd been a minor prospect himself early on as he built up a 12-2 record, even being named "Prospect of the Month" in *The Ring* magazine back in 1953.

He'd taken a five-year break from boxing, during which time he moved to West Virginia and became the youngest police chief in state history. The police department in Fayetteville had just two officers and was so small it didn't even have its own phone, so Hunsaker had to take calls at a phone booth outside the Ben Franklin five-and-dime store.

Hunsaker took time off from boxing but never got it out of his system, so he put on the gloves again in 1958 and quickly ran his record to 17-3-1. That's when he stepped up in class to face Ernie

Terrell, a future heavyweight champ who outlasted Hunsaker for a unanimous decision.

That was the first of six straight losses for Hunsaker leading up to his fight with Clay. Six months before his fight with the former Olympian, he'd been stopped by then-unbeaten Tom McNeeley, who would hit the canvas 11 times in an unsuccessful challenge to Floyd Patterson a year later.

Still, Hunsaker had reason to be confident: He'd only been stopped twice — once by McNeeley in the ninth round, and the other time after being butted in the nose — and had been in the ring against seasoned veterans, while Clay was still extremely green.

"I have fought men whose record proved that Cassius Clay shouldn't even be in the same town as them," he wrote to a friend, predicting a knockout.

Larry Boeck of the *Louisville Courier-Journal*, meanwhile, wrote that Hunsaker didn't "appear to be a safe pushover." He was "no Sonny Liston... but he hasn't been dug out of the graveyard at midnight, either, and propped up on a Halloween broom to furnish Clay a target to shoot at."

Despite the hype, the fight was far from a sellout. A crowd of just 6,100 assembled for the card at 20,000-seat Freedom Hall in Louisville, even though the proceeds went to a children's hospital, with fans paying $2, $3.50, or $5, and students getting in for a dollar.

The fight itself was lopsided and largely forgettable: Clay dominated with his quickness, bloodying Hunsaker's nose in the third round and opening a cut over his eye in the fourth. But it went the full six rounds without a knockdown or any significant damage to either man. The judges gave Clay all six rounds, scoring the fight 30-24, 30-23, and 30-19.

Clay dismissed Hunsaker after the fight, saying, "The Tunney

Hunsaker I fought was too easy — I was fresher after the fight than I was before."

Hunsaker, on the other hand, praised Clay.

"He's awfully good for an 18-year-old and as fast as a middleweight," he said. "The kid can be heavyweight champions of the world someday. He's that good, if he settles down to hard work."

Clay got $2,000 for the fight, while Hunsaker pocketed $300.

The two men didn't see each other again for 27 years, until a now-retired Ali agreed to appear for an autograph-signing session in Charleston to promote the Golden Gloves program. Hunsaker was invited to join the former champ, and the pair posed for cameras, trading fake punches.

The event was a hit, and they re-created it several times over the next few years. Ali even visited Hunsaker's hometown in 1992, visiting with special needs children on a passing school bus and stopping at a local flower shop. The occasion? Hunsaker was retiring as Fayetteville police chief.

He had been serving for 38 years.

Crime

Burglars cracked the safe at the Coyle & Richardson Department Store, making off with about $6,000. Police saw no sign of forced entry, leading them to believe that the criminals had concealed themselves inside the store at closing time.

Once everyone had gone, the burglars forced their way into the fourth-floor vault and stacked mattresses they got from the same floor of the store against the doors. They were therefore able to stifle the noise they made as the proceeded to break into the large safe, which measured 6 feet high and 4 feet wide.

They punched and sawed out the combination of the outer door to access the interior, which contained a smaller safe with

$5,000 and a petty cash box with $1,000 more.

Lt. W.W. Fisher, a detective on the case, called the safecracking "about as professional a job as we've ever had in Charleston."

A couple of weeks later, a pair of ex-convicts were arrested in another case that police called similar to the heist at Coyle's: a break-in at Stonewall Jackson High School.

A detective caught them red-handed, and they admitted breaking into two other schools, taking about $100 from a safe at Buffalo High in Putnam County and more than $700 from a safe in Dunbar County. Both safes had been cut open using a blowtorch. The pair also admitted to other thefts in the area, but denied being involved in the Coyle's job.

Milestones

The 1950s and the Baby Boom marked the final decade of population growth in Charleston, as a 16.7 percent surge sent the city to an all-time high of 85,796.

Music

Louis Armstrong brought his trumpet to the Charleston Civic Center on July 14. Tickets were $2.50 in advance or $2.75 at the door.

1961

Baseball

The Charleston Senators were history, but a new team filled the void when the San Juan Marlins of the AAA International League moved to Charleston on May 19 after just 27 games.

The Marlins finished the season in second place at 88-66 and qualified for the championship series, but were swept by the third-place Buffalo Bisons in four games during the first round of the playoffs.

The Charleston Marlins didn't last beyond the season's end, though.

Disaster

It was already the wettest July on record when a new storm hit the city on the 19th that made everything that had come before pale by comparison. A deluge of 6 inches of rain was dumped on the area in four hours, which was more than mountain creeks could handle.

Walls of water 15 feet high swept down through populated hollows, breaking up and sweeping away houses on the hills around town, as 22 people died in the flood and two more in a landslide. Two hundred other people found themselves homeless in the storm, which did an estimated $4 million in damage.

A creek called Magazine Branch that ran parallel to Garrison Avenue in Magazine Hollow turned into a vicious torrent that demolished more than a dozen homes and took nine lives. More damage was done by Elk Two-Mile and Campbell's creeks.

Clide Hart, 69, and his wife Sophie, 53, watched in horror as their home was ripped from its foundation and crushed their 10-year-old daughter, Nancy Lou, to death against a neighboring home on Garrison Avenue.

"I opened the front door, and that's when the water got us," said Clide Hart, who had been born disabled. "I told Nancy to get hold of her mother's hand but she jumped off the bed instead, and that's the last we saw of her."

Hart and his wife became separated when the rushing water wedged him between a tree trunk and a two-by-four, where he was stuck for three hours before being rescued. The couple were reunited hours later at Union Mission.

Herbert Waugh went to a neighbor's home on Garrison because he was worried about a young boy there who had been left disabled by polio. He gathered the child into his arms and started wading through the water, just ahead of the boy's mother and her other son. But the next time he looked around, they had vanished.

The bodies of Patricia Byers, 48, and Ricky Byers, 9, were found later.

A fourth-grade student named Sherry Lynn Givens drowned when waters swept into her home on Garrison, where press accounts described a "bizarre scene" littered with washing machines, refrigerators, broken utility lines, dolls, a mattress, lavatories, and about 50 twisted cars. A pair of false teeth was also found lying in the mud.

Ten feet of water flooded the basement of an office building across the street from the Statehouse.

At Elk Two-Mile, Fred Wooten, 60, drowned when he fell from the roof of his home, where he was stranded along with his wife, son, daughter-in-law, and two grandchildren. His son Clyde also fell along with his 4-year-old daughter, but they managed to escape with minor injuries by grabbing a tree where they remained perched all night.

Nine houses were washed away on Elk Two-Mile.

"The water was almost to the porch when we started up the hill," one resident said. "I packed my son-in-law right up there. We used the kids' plastic swimming pool, stuck up on four poles, as shelter. We didn't come back till nearly dawn."

On Washington Street, the operator of the Night Owl Superette drowned when he stepped out of his car and was dragged underneath it.

Retail

There was a time when toys were more than just video games, and the Fountain Hobby Center had plenty of choices for kids (and grown-ups) who wanted something more than the latest doll or wagon.

The store on Washington Street had science and chemistry kits for sale, with refills, and microscopes to boot. If science wasn't your thing, you could

The Fountain Hobby Center on Washington Street. *Author photo*

find stamp albums, mosaic tile kits, paint-by-number sets, model aircraft, art supplies, and model railroads.

And yes, they had regular toys, too. A January sale offered a $20 giant doll house for just $12.99, a Chatty Kathy talking doll for $11.99 instead of the regular $17.95, and pump-action Daisy air rifles for under $7, and Parker Bros.' Risk game for under $5.

1962

Baseball

Charleston got another new team, a Cleveland Indians affiliate called, not too originally, the Indians in the AA Eastern

League.

Tommie Agee, who would go on to a 12-year career in the majors, was among the players on the Charleston roster. So were pitchers Tommy John and Luis Tiant, both of whom would later pitch in the World Series. (John even had a surgical procedure named after him.)

Neither one of them managed a winning record in Charleston, though. The ace of the staff was another future big-leaguer, Sonny Siebert, who went 15-8 with a 2.91 ERA and 192 strikeouts.

The team finished fifth in the six-team league, but won the pennant the following year with an 83-57 record. Tommy John was a standout again, going 9-2 with an ERA of 1.61 ERA, but saw limited action in Charleston because he pitched 25 games in the majors that year.

The Indians played one more season in Charleston, finishing fourth in 1964.

Jean Carson appearing in "Frontier Doctor."

Television

Charleston's own Jean Carson made her first of four appearances on *The Andy Griffith Show*, playing Jalene Naomi Connors in an episode titled "Convicts at Large."

She would return to the show three more times, but in a different role, that of Daphne, one of the flirtatious "fun girls" from Mount Pilot. (Joyce Jameson played the other "fun girl," Skippy.)

Carson played a number of other roles on television in the 1950s and early '60s, appearing as a guest on such notable shows as *Perry Mason*, *The Twilight Zone*, *The Untouchables*, *Sugarfoot*, and *Death Valley Days*.

Her final film role was in the 1977 movie *Fun with Dick and Jane*. She died in 2005.

1963

Fast Food

"Bigger Better Faster," was the motto of the new burger joint in town.

Burger Boy Food-O-Rama was a rapidly expanding fast-food chain based in Columbus, which ventured beyond the Ohio state line for the first time in March by opening a restaurant in Oak Hill. The business was just two years old, but it was growing quickly. In 1963 alone, it opened six restaurants in West Virginia, including one in Charleston at 213 MacCorkle Ave.

(The others were in St. Albans, Huntington — which had two — and Parkersburg.)

Two more Burger Boy outlets would be built in Charleston in 1965: at 1302 Bigley Ave. and at the corner of Third Avenue and Patrick Street, an intersection most recently occupied by Rally's, Taco Bell, and McDonald's.

The city's first Burger Boy opened just a year after Burger Chef opened South Charleston, offering burgers, shakes, and fries for 15 cents each. Burger Boy matched those prices for burgers and fries, offering shakes for 20 cents, while also serving fish sandwiches for a quarter and tubs of chicken with a dozen pieces for $1.99.

Roast beef was a big draw, too, and there was a double cheeseburger called the Giant that eventually morphed into a triple-decker. Unlike some early fast-food restaurants, which just had walk-up windows, at least some BBFs had indoor seating, and one in Huntington had miniature jukeboxes at the tables.

There was also a catchy jingle that began:

Everybody's goin' to a BBF, and taking their appetite.
Everybody's goin' to a BBF at the whirling satellite.

The "whirling satellite" was a multicolored sign in the form of a starburst, with neon tubes shooting out in all directions from the center.

But not everyone liked it. In fact, residents of Beckley started complaining that the satellite sign there was interfering with their TV reception, and air-traffic controllers worried that it might be causing problems for flight signals, as well. The problem, fortunately, appears to have been solved by a technician about a week later.

In all, a total of 48 Burger Boy outlets had opened in Ohio, West Virginia, and Kentucky by 1970, at which point they were sold to Borden. Some continued under the Burger Boy name for a time, while at least one eventually switched over to Borden Burger. Now, BBF stood for Borden's Better Foods.

Milton Lustnauer, who cofounded the original chain, went on to own several Wendy's and Long John Silvers locations.

For the record, the entire jingle went:

Everybody's goin' to a BBF, and taking their appetite.
Everybody's goin' to a BBF at the whirling satellite.
You can eat 'em there, or take 'em home,
And entertaining can be fun.
Let BBF be your party chef.
Serve a banquet on a bun!

1964

Civil Rights

Rock Lake Pool was *the* place to be during the summer.

Newspaper reports in the 1930s said the pool drew 2,000 people in a day on more than one occasion, and in at least one instance as many as 4,000. But none of those swimmers were Black: The pool remained segregated through the 1950s and into the '60s.

In 1964, the West Virginia State chapter of the Congress of Racial Equality (CORE) started calling for protests and, then, a boycott of the pool. The boycott came in response to Joe Wilan's refusal to integrate the pool on the grounds that it would be bad for business.

Rock Lake Pool contained 2.9 million gallons of water and featured attractions like a trapeze and trampoline. But until the late 1960s, only whites were allowed to use it. *enrichyourmind, Creative Commons 3.0*

CORE chapter president Robert Parkins issued the following statement: "It is the opinion of Mr. Wilan, the owner of Rock Lake Pool, that the citizens of Kanawha County will not support his pool if it is integrated. If you, the citizens of Kanawha County, comply with our plea, we may prove Mr. Wilan wrong without demonstration."

Joe Wilan said he had figures to back up his assertion: He rented a county voting machine and hired a county voter registration worker to operate it. Then he posed the question: "Would you continue coming to swim at Rock Lake Pool if Negroes were admitted?"

The results, according to Wilan, were 493 no and just 80 yes.

"We were under enormous pressure from white people" Sam Wilan said later. "We were running a business, not a social experiment."

When the boycott failed to prove CORE's point, protests followed. Some protesters formed a human wall to block the ticket window, while others waited all day in line. When they got to the front, they would be turned away. Then they'd go to the back of the line and start all over again.

When 100 protesters showed up to picket outside the pool in August of 1965, the owner turned water hoses on them. A judge intervened to stop that. But the following week, protesters were met with a barbed-wire fence. Black protesters were turned away, and so were white protesters who admitted to being part of the group.

The picketing continued that summer and the following year, as well.

In the end, it took the passage of the West Virginia Human Rights Act in 1967 to force the pool's integration. Joe Wilan had tried to get around the law by selling memberships to convert the pool into a private facility, but he couldn't sell enough of them to turn a profit.

Homer Davis, state director of the NAACP, was a key figure in pushing for the pool to integrate. Once that was accomplished, he said, it was a watershed moment for the civil rights movement in Kanawha County.

"It had the effect of opening up the whole valley," he said. "After that, we didn't have any problems with discrimination in public places."

The Wilans would continue to operate the pool until 1985.

Football

Charleston had a pro football team.

It wasn't in the NFL or AFL, but the United Football League, a Midwest-based circuit entering its third season with ambitions of going national.

The UFL already had one team in West Virginia, the Wheeling Ironmen, who had won the championship in each of their first two seasons. And the Ironmen — specifically, Bob Ferguson from the team's board of directors — were instrumental in bringing pro football to Charleston.

"I was visiting in Wheeling, my wife's home town, last Christmas Eve when Bob Ferguson first raised the question," said Charleston attorney William T. Lively Jr., who became instrumental in the drive to add Charleston to the UFL. "He spoke of the success the Ironmen were having, and of how the natural rivalry between Wheeling and Charleston would be good for both cities."

Things went quickly from there. Lively got a follow-up call from the UFL commissioner five days later, and less than two months after Ferguson first broached the idea, the Charleston franchise was approved. Fifty-three shareholders gobbled up $40,000 worth of stock.

Alex Schoenbaum, former Ohio State football star and owner of the Shoney's restaurant chain, topped the list.

Other teams in the eight-team league included the Canton Bulldogs (named after the iconic NFL team) and Toledo Tornadoes in Ohio, Grand Rapids Blazers in Michigan, Joliet Chargers in Illinois, and Indianapolis Warriors. The Chargers, the last team to join the league that year, went winless in 14 games.

The league also included the first Canadian team ever to play American pro football, the Quebec Rifles, who played in 20,000-seat Delormier Downs. The Rockets and Rifles would make history when they met in a preseason exhibition before 8,400 fans at the Downs on Aug. 23. The Rockets prevailed 35-19.

It was already clear that Perry Moss, a former star quarterback at the University of Illinois who had been was hired as the Rockets' head coach and general manager, was building a solid team.

"We don't expect to win the championship the first season," Lively said. "But we do expect to field a representative team that will provide a really professional, crowd-pleasing brand of football."

The Rockets more than met those expectations.

On September 6, Charleston and Wheeling met at Wheeling Island Stadium before a near-capacity crowd of almost 11,000 fans, the largest crowd to see a UFL game that season.

Charleston quarterback Ron Miller connected with 5-foot-9 split end Sam Weir on two touchdown strikes in the first quarter, covering 23 and 79 yards. That proved to be enough against the Ironmen, as the Rockets came away with a 20-9 victory.

The Rockets would beat the Ironmen again in Charleston 28-23 on Halloween and rolled up a six-game winning streak heading into the final game of the season against Toledo. That stretch included an 82-7 demolition of the Grand Rapids Blazers in which the Rockets scored 34 points in the second quarter alone. Wilburn Hollis scored five touchdowns, and Charleston quarterbacks Miller and Ron Pennington combined for nine TD passes, with Miller throwing six of them.

But less than two weeks later, in the season's final game, the Rockets' offense was nowhere to be found in a 10-3 upset loss to the Toledo Tornadoes.

That loss proved costly.

Even though Charleston finished with the second-best record in the league at 11-3, the Rockets finished behind the Canton Bulldogs in the Western Division and failed to qualify for the championship game, where the Canton beat the Indianapolis Warriors 19-14.

Miller threw for 3,202 yards and 25 touchdowns on the year, while Weir finished with 13 touchdowns on 1,089 yards receiving. Dual-purpose back Hollis, meanwhile, wound up with 648 yards rushing and 618 receiving, crossing the goal line a dozen times.

But none of them was the biggest name on the roster. That honor belonged to a 6-foot-4 defensive end and lineman out of Jackson State named Coy Bacon. The 21-year-old would play three seasons for the Rockets and another for the Orlando Panthers of the Continental Football League before finally catching on in the NFL, where he played 14 years.

Bacon, a three-time Pro Bowler, led the NFL in sacks in 1976 and racked up 130 for his career with the Los Angeles Rams, San Diego, Cincinnati, and Washington.

As for the Rockets, the best was yet to come.

In their five-year history, they'd endure just one losing season, finishing with an overall mark of 49-18-0 during that span. Moss would find the greatest success with the team, losing just three times as a coach in 28 starts. Years later, during the 1990s, he would find more success coaching the Orlando Predators in the Arena Football League.

Music

The same week in late January/early February saw Peter, Paul and Mary perform at the Civic Center and John Lee Hooker appear at the Malibu Club, 5630 MacCorkle Ave. in Kanawha City.

1965

Laidley Field was home to the Charleston Rockets of the Continental Football League. *Author photo*

Football

Everyone remembers the 1972 Miami Dolphins as the only undefeated team in modern pro football history.

But that's not quite true.

Just seven years earlier, the Charleston Rockets had already done it.

The Rockets were no longer in the United Football League. Charleston joined four other teams from the UFL and four teams from the Atlantic Coast Football League to create the Continental Football League.

Wheeling moved over from the UFL, giving the new league two natural rivals in West Virginia. The former Canton team moved to Philadelphia, while the Quebec Rifles transferred to

Toronto and the Indianapolis Warriors shifted to Fort Wayne.

The four teams that joined from the ACFL were Hartford, Richmond, Newark, and Springfield, Mass. The Springfield franchise moved to Norfolk, Virginia before the season started, and another team was added in Providence, Rhode Island to create a new 10-team circuit that was meant to challenge the NFL and AFL as a third major league.

"We're going to have the best pro league in the United States and Canada," said Sol Rosen, general manager of the Newark Bears. However he may have meant that, it was accurate: The Continental Football League was, in fact, the *only* football league with teams in *both* the United States and Canada.

To add credibility to their venture, the owners hired Happy Chandler as the league's commissioner: The two-term governor of Kentucky also had served for six years as commissioner of Major League Baseball.

The Rockets had to feel they were in good position to challenge for the title, but it's unlikely that anyone expected how good they would be. They provided a preview by winning exhibition games against Newark and Fort Wayne soundly, then proceeded to reel off 14 wins in a row during the regular season without a defeat.

The only games decided by seven points or less were on consecutive weeks in mid-October: an inexplicably difficult 9-6 win against the league-worst Charter Oaks at Hartford and a 14-7 triumph at home over Fort Wayne.

Highlights were a 31-0 pasting of the league's second-best team, the Toronto Rifles, on the road midway through the season and a 58-21 shellacking of the third-best team, the Philadelphia Bulldogs, also on the road. The latter game was played before the largest crowd to see a Rockets game that season, 13,239 at Temple Stadium.

Overall, on the season, the Rockets scored more points and allowed fewer than any other team in the league, beating their opponents by an average tally of 33-9. They were so much better than everybody else that the championship game — a rematch with Toronto at Charleston's Laidley Field — was anticlimactic. The Rifles actually managed to score a touchdown this time, but the Rockets still won going away, 24-7 before a home crowd of 7,105.

Quarterback Ron Miller hit Jim Moss on a 29-yard touchdown pass and scored himself on an 8-yard run to give Charleston a 14-0 lead at halftime, while the Rockets held the Rifles scoreless through three quarters.

Joe Williams, the league's leading rusher, supplied Toronto's only score on a 43-yard run in the fourth period. But the Rockets kept Toronto pinned deep in its own territory most of the game, thanks to Jim Hollingsworth, who boomed second-half punts of 75, 89 (yes, 89), 49, and 65 yards.

On the season, the team's balanced attack was led by Millard Fleming, who caught a team-leading 42 passes for 520 yards and also rushed for 501 yards. Ron Miller took most of the snaps at quarterback, throwing for 1,866 yards and 21 touchdowns with 11 interceptions.

The Rockets placed three players on the all-league offensive team: linemen Carl Robinson and Arlen Cullors, and tight end Jim Moss. Five more made the defensive team: end Bill Miller, tackle Joe Critchlow, linebacker Sam Fernandez, cornerback Mike FitzGerald, and safety Roger McFarland. Placekicker Eddie Mitchamore and punter Hollingsworth also made the team. Mitchamore made 54 of 56 extra points and was the league's most accurate field goal kicker at 63 percent. Hollingsworth, meanwhile, averaged 44 yards a punt to lead the league.

Music

ABC's musical television show *Shindig!* had premiered in 1964, featuring musical performances by a Sam Cooke, the Everly Brothers, The Who, Little Eva, and the Rolling Stones, among others.

In May of 1965, the show took its act on the road and came to the Charleston Civic Center with a pair of Friday night shows featuring host Jimmy O'Neill at 7:30 and 10:15 o'clock. Gerry & the Pacemakers, an early British Invasion act, were the headliners, with Shirley Ellis second on the bill.

Others set to take the stage were The Dixie Cups, Willie Nelson, Linda Gail, Joey Paich, and Jim Doval & the Gauchos. Football star Roosevelt "Rosey" Grier was an extra added attraction.

Tickets were, $2, $2.50, and $3 for all-reserved seating and could be purchased at Galperin Music, Sears, Turners, and the Civic Center.

1966

Basketball

Wilt Chamberlain made history in Charleston, scoring 41 points for the Philadelphia 76ers in a 149-123 victory over the Detroit Pistons at the Civic Center.

Five thousand fans turned out in Charleston to watch Chamberlain surpass Bob Pettit as the NBA's all-time leading scorer, with 20,844 points. He scored 19 points in the fourth quarter and set the record on a free throw with 1:32 left.

Civil Rights

Integration didn't happen overnight, and it wasn't happening at the Skateland roller rink — at least not if the owner, Margaret

Tucker, had anything to say about it.

On a Friday night in mid-March, a group of 18 members from the NAACP youth council made their way to the business at 710 Virginia St. They'd chosen the business because it was one of the few places in the city that offered recreational facilities for children.

But Tucker had other priorities.

"I'm not going to have my business ruined," she declared in turning them away. "I'm not going to mix the races and have the tension."

She was worried about her own self-interest, too. She said mothers left their children in her care for two or three hours, and she feared that she could be accused of discrimination if she tried to keep a Black child from "getting out of line" by telling him or her what to do.

Besides, she said, "I don't feel whites and blacks are ready to mix socially."

And she had letters to back up her position from a pair of lawmakers: U.S. Sen. Robert Byrd and U.S. Rep. John Slack and. Byrd, a former member of the KKK who would become the nation's longest-serving senator, was adamant: "Based on the facts which appear in your correspondence, there is no way you can be forced to admit Negroes," his letter read.

But the NAACP group disagreed. They planned to picket, citing the 1964 Civil Rights Act, while also addressing other issues in the community such as reports of discrimination against drum majorettes and cheerleaders.

The rink, however, was an important test.

In February of 1967, local judge John Charnock handed down the first ruling in such a case, stating his opinion that Skateland and similar businesses were not places of public accommodation under the Civil Rights Act. That meant the owner, Tucker, was within her rights to admit some members of the public while denying admission to others.

But the judge's opinion didn't matter for long, because as Granville Reed of the NAACP pointed out, Tucker's stance was not only out of step with the Civil Rights Act, but with the overall atmosphere in Charleston. He was proved correct when West Virginia passed a state human rights act that required the integration of businesses like Skateland.

Tucker's response?

She closed the business as of June 1, 1967, a month before the new human rights act was scheduled to take effect.

"It's been proved all over the country in the skating rink business that when Negroes enter a skating rink, whites leave," she said. "After the white business drops off, the Negroes have no desire to skate by themselves. That leaves the rink owner with no business at all.

"I have nothing against the Negro race," she continued. "I'd rather just close up my rink without seeing it die a slow death."

She said she had operated another skating rink in town for African-American patrons, employing an all-Black staff, at the Kanawha and Elk rivers.

"I got along fine with Negroes and even sold the business to one of them who helped me," she said, reiterating that she had no quarrel "with Negroes, of whom many are fine, upstanding people." However, she added that she believed the new law to be one-sided and discriminatory against private business owners.

It "strips away their rights, and prevents them from operating their business, in which they've invested their money and lives, in a manner which they believe will be to the best interests of that business," she said.

The rink welcomed 75 skaters for its final night of operations. After that, Tucker put the 190-by-60-foot portable building that housed it up for sale. An A&P Supermarket was built in its place, and as of 2021, the site housed a Save a Lot market.

Tucker and her husband John, meanwhile, moved to Fort Myers, Florida, where they operated a real estate company.

Fast Food

A&W Root Beer had started out on the West Coast, in Lodi, California, to be precise, but it was awfully popular in Charleston.

So popular that, by the fall of 1966, there were four drive-in locations in the area — on Morris Street, MacCorkle Avenue, Central Avenue, and Virginia Street next to the Arcade — plus the snack bar in Elk City Lanes at Ohio Avenue and Lee Street.

A&W was offering a weekend special of four giant barbecue sandwiches plus a half-gallon jug of root beer for $1.79.

Hot dogs were popular in West Virginia, so A&W obliged by serving those, too. A few years later, they offered what they called a "Frank 'n' Stein Special," that gave you a free 8-ounce stein of root beer when you purchased a Coney Island hot dog. Root beer floats were also on the menu, but if you preferred plain soft-serve ice cream, Charleston had a Dairy Queen, too, on Central Avenue at Russell Street.

Of course, you could still buy burgers at A&W, which was home to the "Burger Family," and there were a couple of Burger Chef restaurants in town, too: You could find them both on MacCorkle Avenue in South Charleston and Kanawha City, respectively. Burger Chef, which for a while ranked second to McDonald's nationally, was a 69-cent deal on two of its Big Shef sandwiches (yes, that's how they spelled that).

Or, if none of that suited your taste, you could drive to one of two Painter's Drive-In locations in the area for a different sort of weekend special: a complete oyster dinner with six fresh oysters, fries, and coleslaw for $1.25. And if seafood wasn't to your liking, you could get boxes, buckets, or barrels of Kentucky Fried Chicken at Painter's, too.

Football

The Charleston Rockets had another good team, but not quite good enough to win a second straight championship. The Orlando Panthers, relocated from Newark, had their number, handing them two of their four losses by narrow margins of 27-24 (in overtime) and 17-13.

Then, in the playoffs, the Panthers won again, although it still wasn't easy. The game was tied 24-24 before Orlando scored the deciding touchdown on a 1-yard plunge by quarterback Don Jonas that capped an 84-yard drive.

Charleston finished the regular season with a 10-4 record, second-best in the league behind Orlando.

The Rockets would slump the next season to 6-8.

1967

Music

The Young Rascals had just had their second No. 1 hit with "Groovin'" a few months before they appeared in concert on a 15-foot-high stage at the Charleston Civic Center for the "First Annual After Football Season Concert."

The second act on the bill was no slouch himself. He wouldn't hit No. 1 himself until three years later with a tune called "Cracklin' Rosie," but he'd already penned a No. 1 hit for someone else: The Monkees' "I'm a Believer," which had topped the charts at the end of December 1966.

Still, Neil Diamond would have a much longer career than the Young Rascals, even though he wasn't as hot at the time. (Diamond would return for a sellout show as a headliner in 1971 and headline another show the following year.)

A ticket priced at $3.50 got you through the turnstiles to see both of them, in addition to a pre-concert "Battle of the Bands" featuring the Majestics, the Marquis, and the Dee-Jays.

1968

Basketball

Charleston High went unbeaten en route to the AAA state title, led by Levi Phillips, Curtis Price, and Larry Harris — each of whom was recruited by West Virginia University.

Price averaged 19.7 points on the season, following a junior year in which he averaged 23.1. Harris, meanwhile, set a state tournament record with 33 rebounds in a 102-75 opening-round win over Wheeling.

The Cougars' 78-64 triumph over Woodrow Wilson of Beckley in the championship avenged a 75-69 loss in the finals a year earlier.

During one stretch spanning two seasons, Charleston would win 48 straight games under coach Lou Romano.

Football

St. Albans wasn't happy.

The school had advanced to the AAA state championship game against Charleston, but the game was scheduled to be played at Laidley Field in Charleston. St. Albans argued that would give the CHS an unfair "psychological advantage."

After all, Charleston had already beaten the Red Dragons once at Laidley during the season, 27-7. On the other hand, however, Charleston had also won at St. Albans, 21-0, the previous year.

Both times, St. Albans had a tough time scoring.

The 1968 title game, which was moved to Parkersburg — 100 miles away from either school, at St. Albans' request — was no different. Charleston High just managed a field goal, but it was enough, as the defense did the rest. CHS downed St. Albans 3-0 to capture the state crown.

It was the first of three in a row, each of them low-scoring affairs. Charleston would defeat Buckhannon-Upshur 6-0 in the 1969 title tilt and duplicate that score in 1970 against Victory. In three consecutive finals, the team never surrendered a single point.

Music

Dick Clark's Caravan of Stars made a stop February 9 at the Municipal Auditorium, headlined by Paul Revere and the Raiders, who'd had seven top-20 hits over the previous three years.

Rounding out the bill for the 2½-hour show were Freddy Cannon, Bryan Hyland & the Jokers, the Exiles, the Chips, and George McCannon the III. Tickets were $2, $3, and $4, or you could wait a couple of weeks and see Eddy Arnold at the Civic Center in his first West Virginia appearance.

Arnold was bringing a 20-piece orchestra and four other acts with him, but prices were the same as for the Dick Clark show.

1969

Football

The Charleston Rockets had flown their last mission. The Continental Football League's only undefeated championship team was calling it quits.

Shoney's owner Alex Schoenbaum had handed the reins to Heck's Department Store owner Fred Haddad after the Rockets' disappointing 6-8 season in 1967, and they'd rebounded to post an 8-3 record the following year. That season had even included a 14-10 win over the eventual league champion Orlando Panthers.

But attendance at Laidley Field had been sparse, failing to top 5,000 on all but two of six home dates even though the Rockets went undefeated at home. And the final road game, at Las Vegas, drew just 1,000 fans.

After the season, Haddad decided he'd had enough. He didn't have time to devote to the team, so he withdrew his sponsorship. The franchise had lost $55,000, and Haddad thought it was two years away from making a profit. That was too long to wait. (He turned out to be right: The entire league folded after the 1969 season.)

With Haddad out of the picture, the league suspended the franchise in January for failing to pay a $5,000 assessment.

"It would be a shame to let it go," said coach Billy Barnes, "but it looks like it's on the way out."

And so it was.

The suspension was permanent, and the Rockets never launched again.

Elvis & Jack Frost

1970–1979

Capitol Street seen from the railroad looking toward the river. *Harry Schaefer, National Archives, July 1973*

1970

Milestones

Charleston had more than 14,000 fewer people in 1970 than it'd had a decade earlier, as the population fell to 71,505.

Roller Derby

The banked-track skaters were at the height of their popularity, and two teams — the marquee Oakland Bay Bombers and the Midwest Pioneers — made a stop in Charleston for a single encounter at the Civic Center.

1971

Baseball

Goodbye, Columbus. Hello, Charleston.

The International League's Columbus Jets, an affiliate of the Pittsburgh Pirates, were pulling up stakes and changing their name to the Charlies.

The team had a solid inaugural season, posting a record of 78-62. That was good for third place and a spot in the playoffs, where they were swept in the first round by the Tidewater Tides.

Richie Zisk and Rennie Stennett, two future longtime big-leaguers, had solid seasons at the plate. Zisk hit .290 with 29 home runs and 109 runs batted in, while Stennett finished the season batting .344.

1972

Music

Ozzy and his minions in Black Sabbath invaded the Charleston Civic Center for a March 31 concert. Reserved tickets were available by mail order for $4, $5, or $6 through something called Charleston's Acid Happening.

If your preference was for more wholesome entertainment, you could catch the Osmonds two days earlier for the same price at the same venue. ...

Elton John brought his band to the Civic Center in November, on the crest of his first big wave of popularity. He'd scored three top-10 hits: "Rocket Man," "Honky Cat," and his first chart-topper, "Crocodile Rock."

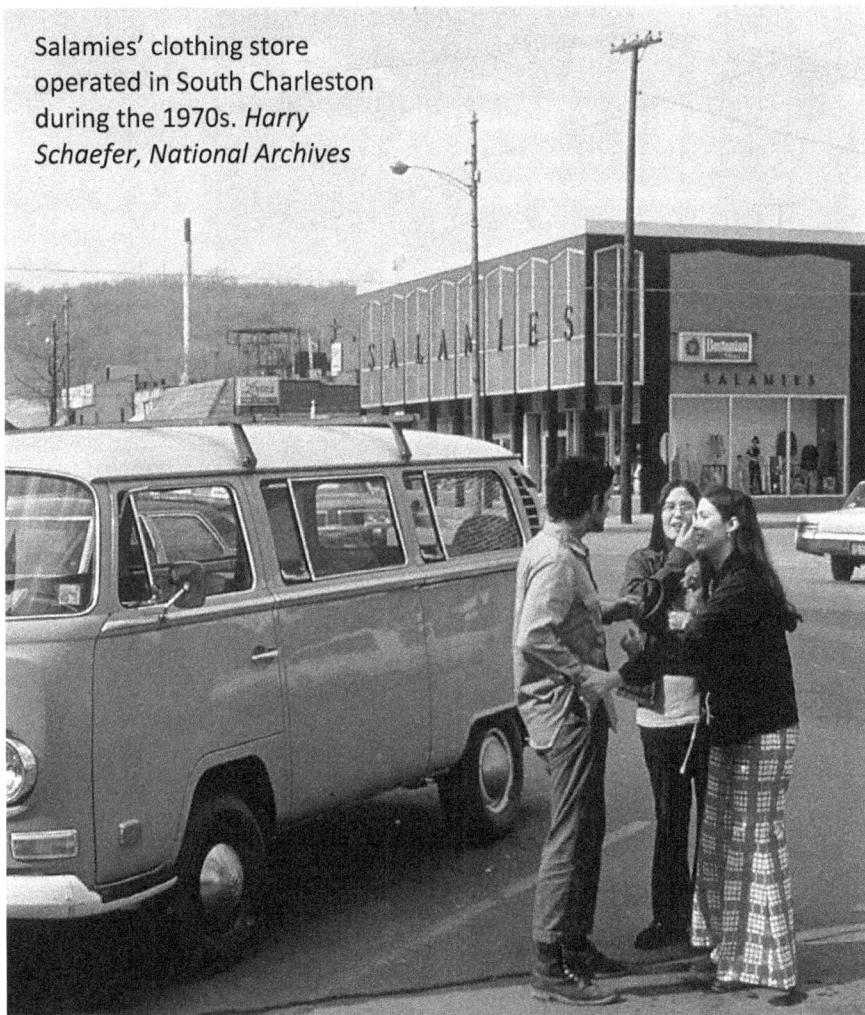

Salamies' clothing store operated in South Charleston during the 1970s. *Harry Schaefer, National Archives*

1973

Basketball

Charleston High completed an unbeaten season on the hardwood to claim the first of two consecutive state titles, going 25-0 and routing Parkersburg 76-56 in the state finals. The 1974 team would go 24-2 and defeat Logan 81-74 for the crown.

A concert on the Capitol steps in 1973 marked Charleston's 110th anniversary. *Harry Schaefer, National Archives*

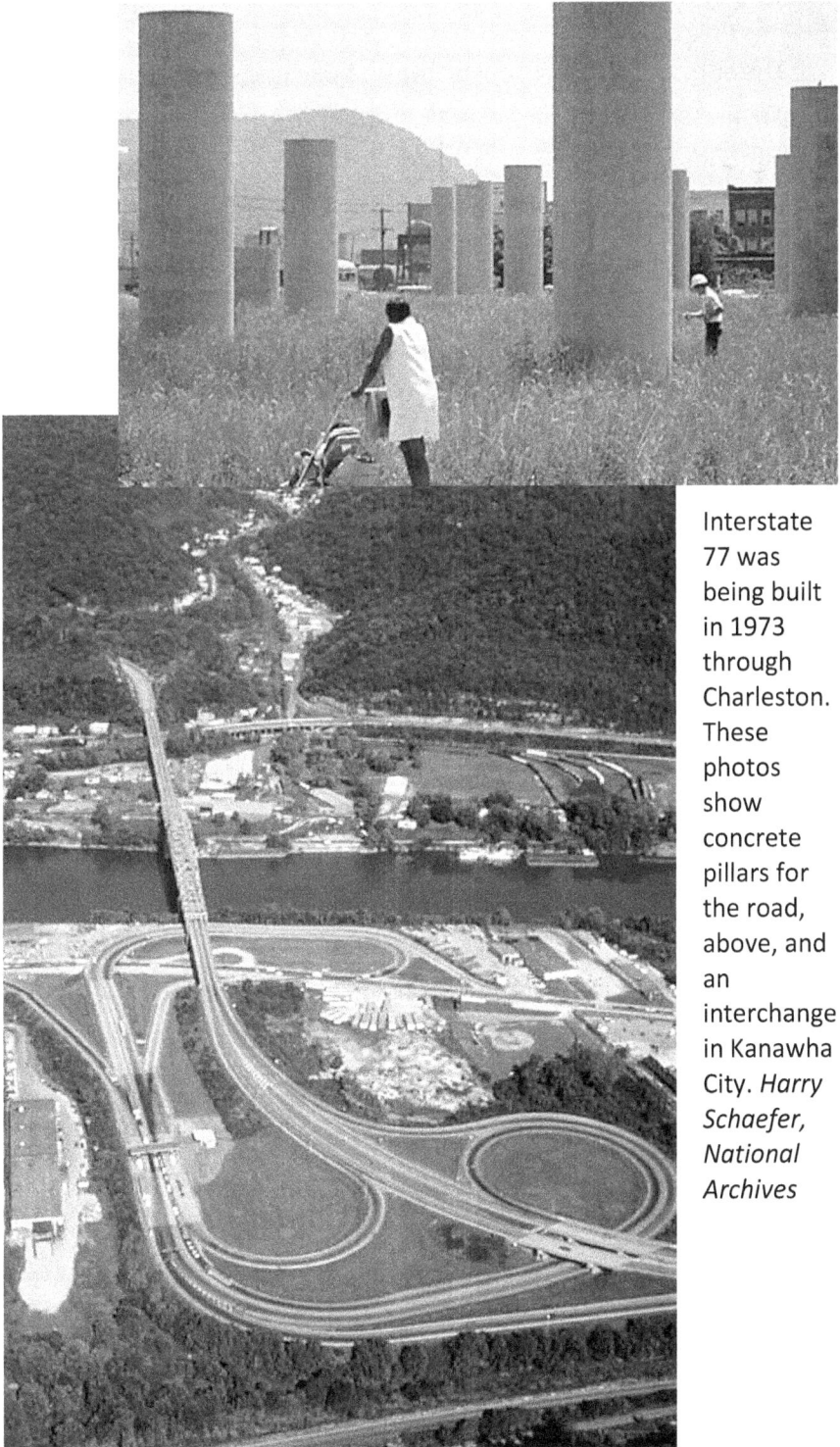

Interstate 77 was being built in 1973 through Charleston. These photos show concrete pillars for the road, above, and an interchange in Kanawha City. *Harry Schaefer, National Archives*

Music

The summer concert season was a busy one, featuring Black Oak Arkansas, John Denver, Glen Campbell, America, Foghat, and the Osmonds.

Downtown Charleston across the Kanawha River in 1973. *Harry Schaefer, National Archives*

1974

Crime

There were five customers inside McCormick Jewelers on Tuesday, June 11, but apparently none of them — nor the employees working there — noticed a heist that was taking place right under their noses.

The thief jimmied open a display window at the Capitol Street business and removed the lock during the late afternoon, making off with three rings worth a total of $14,000. The store owners told police that a couple entered the store together about

4:30 p.m., and the woman apparently distracted a clerk while the man opened the lock.

The lock itself was undamaged, leading police to suspect the heist was the work of a lock artist. But the mechanism apparently wasn't that secure, because a detective was able to re-create the crime by opening it himself in just a few seconds.

Football

Stonewall Jackson High School won its first state championship in decisive fashion, shutting down Parkersburg by a score of 16-0.

Music

David Bowie headlined a summer concert season featuring Frankie Valli and the Four Seasons, Bachman-Turner Overdrive, Ronnie Milsap, and the Hudson Brothers.

Retail

Jack Estep opened Estep's the Nu Look on Lee Street East, but he'd been there a lot longer than that.

Estep had started out as an associate at Moskin's Clothing at the same location when he was just 16 years old. The store changed its name to Calvin's in 1964, and when the store closed a decade later, Estep bought it.

Estep's started out selling clothing for men and women before switching to a focus exclusively on men's clothing in 1986. The store remained open as of 2021.

Estep's is still open today in its original location, more than a half-century after Jack Estep started there. *Author photo*

1975

Fire

During the 1960s and '70s, downtown movie houses fell on hard times as new multiplexes began to take most of their business. They simply couldn't compete by showing the same first-run movies you could see in the suburbs, so some shut down while others searched for alternate programming.

Most of the time, that came in the form of adult movies. Many once-renowned movie houses turned to seamy films that attracted a certain clientele as a way to keep the doors open and the projectors running.

The Lyric Theater was among them, and as of 1971, business was booming.

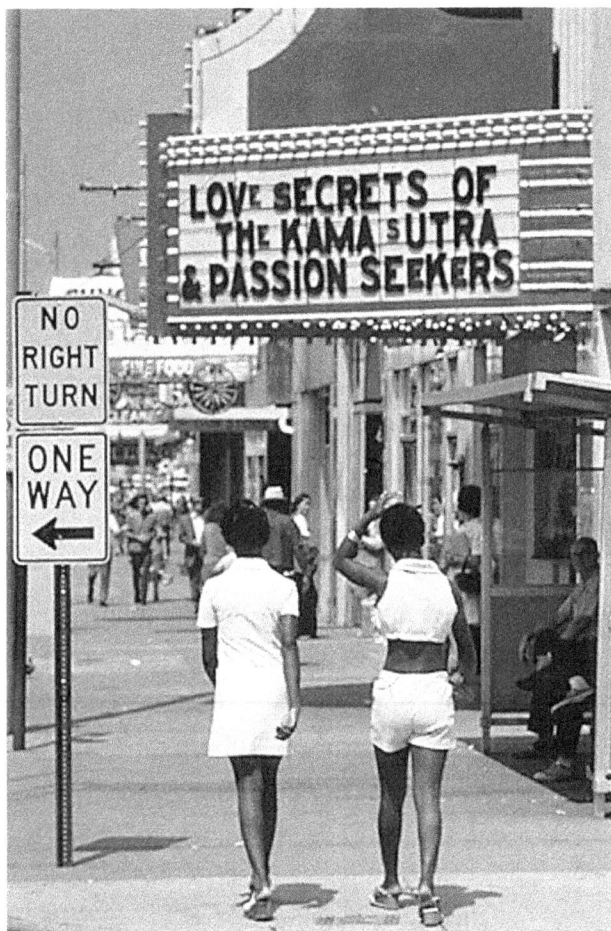

Pedestrians walk past the marquee for the Lyric on Summers Street in 1973. *Harry Schaefer, National Archives*

The Daily Mail reported that the Lyric's exclusively X-rated showings were drawing "near-capacity crowds" to afternoon showings. Manager Lydia Bowring said she'd tried to show Disney movies there for a dollar a ticket, but no one was buying. Sales were far better for the theater's adult offerings.

"We get lawyers, doctors and other professional people in here and we don't have to tie their hands and drag them off the streets to do it," Bowring quipped. She said the theater had made a comeback financially since ditching its western-movie standards for steamier fare.

"Now it's not a booming business, but it is a living, and I'm not ashamed of it."

Some people, however, most certainly were.

In 1969, officers seized a film called *The Secret Sex Lives of Romeo and Juliet* on the grounds that it violated a local obscenity ordinance. But a judge labeled the ordinance "vague at best" and ordered the film returned to the theater. Then, in 1972, the theater agreed to stop showing a film called *Parlor Games* in exchange for having obscenity charges dropped.

But though censors couldn't stop the Lyric from showing "skin flicks," something else did: Fire.

The fire in the wee hours of the morning in late November actually started in another business on Summers Street, the Chicago Meat Market. It spread to the adjacent Lyric within minutes and also engulfed another business, Curly's Men's Shop, on the other side. To make matters worse, Curly's had just brought in extra stock for the Christmas shopping season. It was all lost.

Damage to the 50-year-old brick buildings and their contents was pegged at $300,000, with the fire blamed on transients (referred to as "winos" in the newspapers of the day) who had built fires to keep warm.

Those who disapproved of the X-rated offerings at the Lyric may even have cheered when it went up in flames in late November 1975, but the owners of the Meat Market and Curly's were despondent.

"There goes a lifetime of work," said the Sophie Wiener, who ran Curly's with her husband. "I worked with my husband there from the day we were married. Our whole lives were in that building. ... All I know is that everything was ruined. When we finally got in the building, the water was up to our thighs and the ceiling was gone."

Chicago Meat Market owner John Allessio lamented, "I had a little gold mine there; now it's gone."

But at least one business survived, though it had to move to a new location. Adult movies would keep on being screened, almost without missing a beat: not at the Lyric, which was ruined, but at the now-vacant Custer theater which had opened in 1938 out on Washington Street West.

The Custer became the New Lyric in 1975, showing adult movies, much to the chagrin of some in the neighborhood. *Author photo*

A mere four days after the Lyric fire, the theater owners were talking about reopening there as the New Lyric. It was a plan that didn't sit too well with some in the neighborhood.

"We need a porno house over here like we need a hole in the head," griped Jack Freeland, president of the West Side

Businessmen's Association.

But Bowring, who was still managing the Lyric, said she and her husband planned to have projectors up and running at the Custer less than a week after the Lyric burned. "I've got a right to make a living," she said. "And by the time we open up, the church service will be over."

Protests were planned, but the New Lyric opened as promised. Even an X-rated movie house like the Lyric followed the old showbiz credo.

The show must go on.

Crime

A shot fired from a .38-caliber pistol near the St. Francis Hotel in San Francisco narrowly missed President Gerald Ford from 40 feet away.

The shooter didn't get a second chance, because Secret Service agent Kenneth Iacovoni dashed across the street and tackled her as Ford ducked into his limo.

The forty-something woman who'd fired the shot was Sarah Jane Moore. Back in 1947, she'd been known as Sarah Jane Kahn. That's the year she graduated from Charleston's Stonewall Jackson High School.

Music

The King was about to hold court.

Elvis Presley inked a deal for an appearance at the Civic Center after two years of negotiations that would net him all the ticket proceeds minus $4,000.

The deal, it was reported, could net Presley as much as $70,000 for his first Charleston appearance (about $356,000 in 2021 dollars).

Ticket prices ran from $5 to $10 for the 8,400-seat venue. The concert opened with "See See Rider" and included hits like "Don't Be Cruel," "Hound Dog," "All Shook Up," and "Burning Love." Elvis closed the show with "Can't Help Falling in Love."

But he didn't end up doing just one show.

Tickets were such a hot commodity that Presley did three full concerts: an evening show on July 11, followed by two shows, in the afternoon and evening, on July 12. All three sold out in 18½ hours, a total of 25,200 tickets.

That added up to $253,000 for Presley.

A King's ransom. ...

The Eagles played the Civic Center on July 30 as part of their One of These Nights tour.

They wouldn't be back for 20 years.

Retail

Woodrums' had a big sale on.

The huge store offered everything from furniture to carpeting, appliances to electronics.

An RCA portable 15-inch color TV was $409.^{95}, and you could still get a black-and-white console television if you wanted to save some money: A 22-inch RCA would set you back $209.^{95} Do you remember 8-tracks? You could get a stereo with an 8-track player for $449.

If you were in the market for a Whirlpool washer, you could save $30 and get one for just under $250. Or you could head up to the fourth floor for deals on furniture from Heritage, Drexel, American of Martinsville, and more.

1976

Music

Aerosmith played Charleston Civic Center for the first time on June 13, but it wouldn't be their last. They'd be back in October of 1978, in 1989, and again in 1994.

.

1977

BASEBALL!

American Legion Nite
TONIGHT 7:30
Rock Concert After Game

CHARLESTON vs. TOLEDO
"Charlies"   "Mud Hens

WATT POWELL PARK

Baseball

The Charleston Charlies (now affiliated with the Houston Astros) won their first International League championship after finishing second during the regular season.

They got hot in the playoffs, though, winning seven times in eight games as they polished off Tidewater 3 games to 1, then swept Pawtucket in four games for the title.

The Charlies would have an even better regular season the following year, finishing first at 85-55 before falling to Richmond in the playoffs.

And as it turned out, 1977 was the high-water mark for the Charlies. They played in Charleston through 1983, but didn't win another championship.

Cinema

Star Wars was opening, but the Capitol Theatre was closing. The 800-seat movie house on Summers Street had opened all the

The Plaza Theatre, aka the Capitol, on Summers Street in 2021. *Author photos*

way back in 1912 as the Plaza Theatre, hosting vaudeville and stage plays.

After a fire in the early twenties, it was remodeled to serve as a movie house. The *Star Wars* premier was the last movie to play there. After that, it was remodeled to serve as a performing arts center for several years, before a church purchased it in 2018.

Music

AC/DC was a popular act in Charleston. The rockers from Australia played the Municipal Auditorium on Nov. 26, then returned less than a month later for a concert at the Civic Center on Dec. 17. They'd be back again at the Civic Center in September of the following year and October of '79.

1978

Baseball

South Charleston captured the state baseball championship with a 6-3 victory over Logan. It was the second of back-to-back titles, following on the heels of a 5-4 win over Ravenswood in '77.

The University of Charleston along the Kanawha River adopted its current name in 1978. *Author photo*

Education

Morris Harvey College changed its name to the University of Charleston.

Weather

For Charlestonians who wished for a white Christmas, perhaps they wished too hard.

Santa may have been on time, but Jack Frost was saving something special for the New Year. During the second week of January, the mercury plunged into the single digits, with up to 10 inches of snow falling at some places in the state. The temperatures stayed low, so that snow didn't melt.

But that was just the beginning.

On January 19, a low-pressure system formed near Florida's panhandle in the Gulf of Mexico. Warmer air was moving in from the Carolinas, and forecasters thought it would temper any snowfall in the Mountain State. And in fact, that's how it worked at the higher elevations.

But the opposite happened in the river valleys: Instead of moderating the cold front, the warmer air pressed it down toward the ground, creating snowfall — and a lot of it. Overnight, while most of Charleston slept, 16.4 inches of snow fell on the city, adding to the 8 inches already on the ground.

By the afternoon of January 20, a full 2 feet of snow was on the ground, a record for the city. And it wasn't just on the ground, either. Roofs collapsed and awnings caved in under the weight of the literally heavy snowfall.

Meanwhile, the city was paralyzed. Buses on their way to and from the airport were stranded. Roads were closed; so were schools and businesses, and they stayed that way for days thanks to what was being called the "Great Blizzard of '78."

January ended up as the snowiest month ever for Charleston

at 39.5 inches, while Huntington set a record as well, at 30.3.

Some of that snow melted with rains that hit a few days before the end of the month, causing flooding along the Little Kanawha River and elsewhere, but a lot of it stuck.

And stuck.

And stuck.

A cold February ensured that snow would stay on the ground almost for the rest of the winter. All of it didn't melt until early March, meaning it was on the ground in some places for 60 or even 65 days in a row.

Smokestacks from an FMC plant rise up over a scene on 7th Avenue looking northeast in South Charleston. The Food Machine and Chemical Corp., based in Philadelphia, was one of several industries operating in the Charleston area during the 1970s. *Harry Schaefer, National Archives*

Downtown Makeover

1980–1989

The Charleston Town Center opened in 1983. *Author photo*

1980

Milestones

Charleston's population dipped again, to fewer than 64,000 residents; the population was smaller now than it had been 40 years earlier.

1982

Basketball

The Stonewall Jackson boys edged South Charleston 62-61 for the state championship, concluding a 22-5 season.

1983

Music

Mountain Stage, a two-hour radio show spotlighting an array of musical styles, made its debut on National Public Radio. The show, which was still on the air as of this writing, is recorded before a live audience, most often at the Culture Center Theater in Charleston. As of 2021, it was hosted by South Charleston native and country music legend Kathy Mattea.

Retail

Montgomery Ward was holding a grand opening sale: six lightbulbs for a dollar, Pampers disposable diapers for $7.99, men's knit sport shirts for $3.99, and a canister of three tennis balls for $1.99.

The occasion?

Wards was opening a brand-new store downtown at the Charleston Town Center.

The enclosed shopping mall was unusual. Most indoor malls were in the suburbs, but this one was opening in the heart of the city. In fact, at 931,000 square feet, it was the largest downtown shopping mall east of the Mississippi. In addition to Ward's, Sears, J.C. Penney, and Kaufmann's (a Pittsburgh-based department store) were the anchors.

Capitol Street. *Author photo*

A three-story waterfall flowed down over granite steps of the mall into a garden courtyard. Shoppers could choose from 130 specialty shops along three brick-tiled passageways, such as LeRoy's and Kay's Jewelers. Glass elevators afforded patrons a view of the mall as they gradually ascended and descended, and skylight ceilings bathed the center in natural light.

The mall took 400 days to build.

But even though the $160 million, three-level shopping center was designed to keep people downtown, merchants in the city's retail core weren't too pleased about it.

"As we figure it, Capitol Street will disintegrate," said David Bass of Bass jewelers, referring to the city's historic retail center. Some had already relocated to the mall, while others, such as the iconic Diamond department store, shut their doors for good.

The Stone & Thomas department store — the only one remaining downtown that wasn't at the mall — invested in a $1 million makeover and extended its business hours in an effort to attract more customers.

"We have to give the shopper as good an opportunity to shop with us as with the new girl in town," said Ted Ambrecht, executive vice president of Stone & Thomas, referring to the mall. Eventually, however, Stone & Thomas would bow to the inevitable and move to the mall itself.

1984

Football

Stonewall Jackson edged Brooke 17-14 for the state crown. Brooke would turn the tables three years later with a 12-0 decision.

Retail

A 40-acre shopping center called Kanawha Mall was open for business.

1985

Basketball

Through 26 games, the Stonewall Jackson boys never faltered, completing an unbeaten season with a 63-57 state title victory over St. Albans. They would repeat as champions the following year with a 73-64 win over Oak Hill.

Swimming

After more than five decades in business and nearly four decades under the ownership of the Wilans brothers, Rock Lake Pool was closed for business. Rising insurance costs and competition from free pools spelled the end.

The pool was partially filled in to create space for a miniature golf course and bumper-boats attraction. A go-kart track was laid out in the parking lot, and the pool house was converted into an indoor arcade and restaurant.

The amusement center, known as Rock Lake Golf and Games, lasted until 2006, when it closed and the land was purchased by Rock Lake Presbyterian Church. The rest of the pool was filled in to create a playground two years later.

Approaching Yeager Airport. *Author photo*

Transportation

Kanawha Airport was renamed Yeager Airport.

1986

Basketball

Charleston had a new basketball team, the Gunners, for the 1986-87 season.

They would be playing in the Continental Basketball Association, a minor league with roots dating all the way back to 1946. It had started out as the Eastern Pennsylvania Basketball League and — because its first season tipped off a couple of months before the NBA did — it claimed to be the nation's oldest basketball circuit.

After two seasons, the league became simply the Eastern Pro Basketball League and, in 1978, changed its name again to the CBA. The league experimented with several innovative (and sometimes weird) rules. It used a 3-point shot long before the NBA did, all the way back in 1964, following the lead of the short-lived American Basketball League.

Later on, it tried out a sudden-death overtime rule, a rule that kept players from fouling out, and a scoring system designed to keep even blowouts competitive. Under this system, teams accumulated three points in the standings for winning a game plus an additional point for each quarter they won. As a result, even teams that lost in lopsided fashion could gain a point in the standings by winning a quarter.

Unfortunately for the Gunners, they didn't win enough games — or quarters — to make much of an impact during any of their three seasons in the league.

The team hired Gerald Oliver as its coach; the 51-year-old Knoxville native had coached the CBA's Maine Windjammers to an

18-30 record the previous season, but that franchise had gone dormant, so Oliver landed in Charleston. Upon being introduced as head coach, he said his top priority was to find players with West Virginia connections.

"If we put out a product that fans can identify with, I think they will support us," he said.

True to his word, the Gunners used the fourth selection in the league's draft to select 6-foot-6 forward James Washington from West Virginia State.

Other players on the roster that first season included forward Dan Ruland, brother of the Philadelphia 76ers' Jeff Ruland. Guard George Almones had averaged 18.7 points a game in Bradenton, Florida, and finished second in the league's rookie of the year balloting the previous season.

The Gunners opened their season with a 98-95 loss to the Cincinnati Slammers on the road, and it didn't get much better from there. They played in a six-team division with teams from Tampa, Albany, Jacksonville, Pensacola, and Savannah, finishing fifth with a record of 20-28.

Almones was the team's star, averaging 22.1 points a game while also leading the team in steals and assists. Guard Lamar Harris nailed 44 3-pointers, shooting at a 38.5 percent clip from beyond the arc.

But Almones was gone the following season and out of basketball after that. The Gunners, who played at the Charleston Civic Center, slumped to 14-40 and finished in last place — losing 17 games in a row at one point — before improving to 20-34 in their final Charleston season, good for another fifth-place finish.

Their final game was a 124-120 loss in Topeka. The franchise moved to Columbus, Ohio, the following season.

Not many people showed up to watch the Gunners during their time in Charleston. Owner Jack Catalano quipped: "Instead of having the announcer introduce the players, I should have had him introduce the fans."

1987

Baseball

The Charleston Wheelers were the newest members of the Class A South Atlantic League, where they finished second in the North Division during their inaugural season. They would win the Division in 1991 with their best record ever (92-50), but would fall to the Columbia Mets a three-game sweep for the championship.

1988

Cinema

The Park Place Cinema 7, right, was open at 600 E. Washington St. By 1999, it had expanded to 11 screens. It remained open as of 2021, featuring stadium seating and wall-to-wall curved screens with Dolby sound.

It added another draw to a downtown bolstered by the Charleston Town Center Mall.

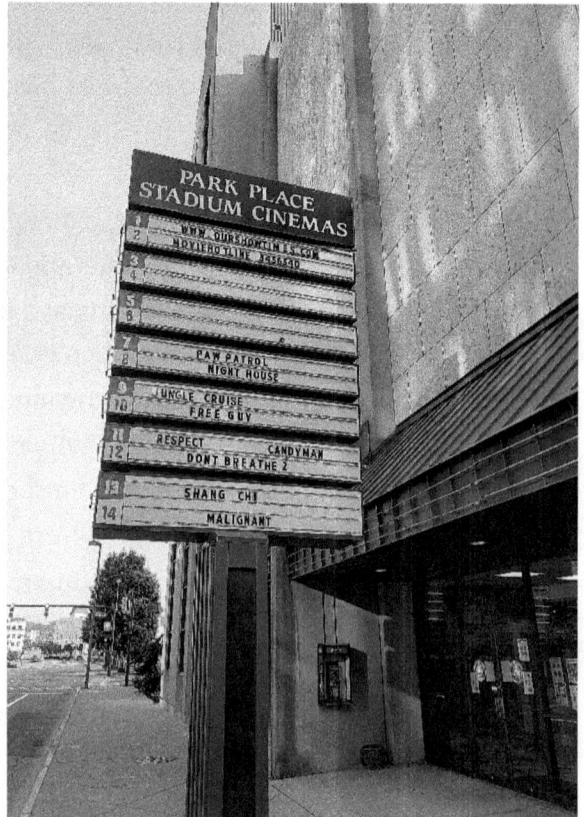

Football

Charleston blanked Greenbrier East 17-0 for the state AAA crown. It had been a while since the Cougars had been in the finals, but it was their fourth consecutive win by shutout in a championship game.

Kathy Mattea in 2000. *John Mathew Smith & www.celebrity-photos.com, Creative Commons 2.0*

Music

South Charleston native Kathy Mattea — the daughter of a chemical plant worker — won the Academy of Country Music and Country Music Association Single of the Year awards for her hit "Eighteen Wheels and a Dozen Roses."

She would also win the ACA song of the year for "Where've You Been" in 1989. The song was inspired by her own grandparents, who were in their 90s when she wrote it.

She would hit the top of the charts with four different singles and make the top 20 with six different albums.

1989

Education

Charleston high school students finally had a new home, but it was far from an easy process.

With the city's population in a long-term decline, the decision had been made to consolidate Charleston and Stonewall Jackson high schools on a single campus. Deciding where that campus should be was the hard part.

It was originally going to be built next to the State Capitol building near Laidley Field, but that idea was nixed because plans were in the works for a Track and Field Hall of Fame there. Those plans never came to fruition, but the high school site search moved on.

It next settled on a site along Greenbrier Street near the airport, but when a plane crashed there, it was seen as too big a risk. So the school board moved the campus five miles out of town on Greenbrier, where it's located today.

Football

The newly consolidated Capital High School didn't waste any time picking up where one of its two processors, Charleston, had left off the year before, downing Brooke 20-13 to capture the state AAA championship.

The Capital High School campus. *Author photo*

End of an Era

1990–1999

A speedboat zips along on the Kanawha River. *Author photo*

1990

Milestones

Another decade of declining population saw Charleston check in at just over 57,000 people, fewer than had lived there in 1930.

1991

Football

Capital High edged Wheeling Park 15-14 for the state AAA title.

1993

The Schoenbaum Stage, named for Shoney's founder Alex Schoenbaum, at the Haddad Riverfront Park Amphitheater. *Author photo*

Community

Haddad Community Park was dedicated downtown beside the Kanawha River, named for Heck's co-founder and president Fred Haddad.

Haddad, who had an office across the river, contributed $500,000 to the park's price tag of $8.5 million, with half the funding coming from the U.S. Army Corps of Engineers. An additional $1.5 million came from private donations raised through the Charleston Renaissance Corp., which sold bricks engraved with donors' names for $50 apiece.

More than three-quarters of the workers involved in the park's construction were from West Virginia.

The venue features a 2,500-seat amphitheater beneath a sail-like canopy overlooking the water, site of concerts and other special events such as car shows, July 4 celebrations, and chili cook-offs. Architect Ed Weber, who designed the canopy, envisioned the park as "the front porch or living room for Charleston."

You can even watch and listen from a boat on the river, or you can just stroll along the riverfront and enjoy the view.

Seating area at the amphitheater, above, and a shaded seating area, right, at Haddad Park. *Author photos*

1994

Football

South Charleston downed University 27-7 for the state title.

1995

Appalachian Power Park would open in 2005. *Author photo*

Baseball

The Charleston Wheelers of the South Atlantic League changed their name to the Charleston Alley Cats. Another name change would take place a decade later, when the team moved into the new Appalachian Power Park and became the West Virginia Power.

Football

Capital High took the state AAA crown with a 20-0 shutout of Hedgeville.

1998

Business

The Arcade's storied 103-year history as a downtown retail hub all came crashing down — thanks to the Hotel Kanawha, which had stood next door for nearly a century.

The sad part is, it didn't have to be that way.

The hotel hadn't been used as for lodging in more than three decades, having closed in 1965, when a pair of local developers came along.

The Job Corps, which had used the building since the hotel closed, had recently moved out, and the developers wanted to spend $20 million and transform it into a boutique hotel. It was an ambitious plan. And, unfortunately, it called for the Arcade be demolished to make way for an underground garage.

So that's what happened: In 1998, the old Arcade was torn down, although the iron trusses that had supported the glass skylight were preserved along with some iron columns to adorn the entrance to the new hotel.

There would be a new ballroom, new rooms, and even a new tower. That was the intent, anyway.

As plans progressed, however, the cost of the project went up. Soon it was half again as expensive, at $30 million, and the developers were having trouble scraping together cash. The parking garage couldn't be built because there wasn't enough land to make it work. So it seems the Arcade had been razed for nothing.

Ultimately, the developers were unable to secure the financing they needed and had to abandon their plans. Another group bought the hotel, but instead of remodeling it, they tore it down.

A new office building went up in its place in 2004.

1999

The Clay Center for the Arts and Sciences is named for Buckner and Lyell Clay, sons of Juliet Staunton Clark. *Author photo*

Community

Construction began on the Clay Center for the Arts and Sciences. It would open in 2003 with an 1,883-seat auditorium, a black-box theater, and the Juliet Art Museum, featuring traveling exhibits.

The Avampato Discovery Museum comprises two floors of interactive science exhibits, along with an art gallery. In all, the center encompasses 240,000 square feet.

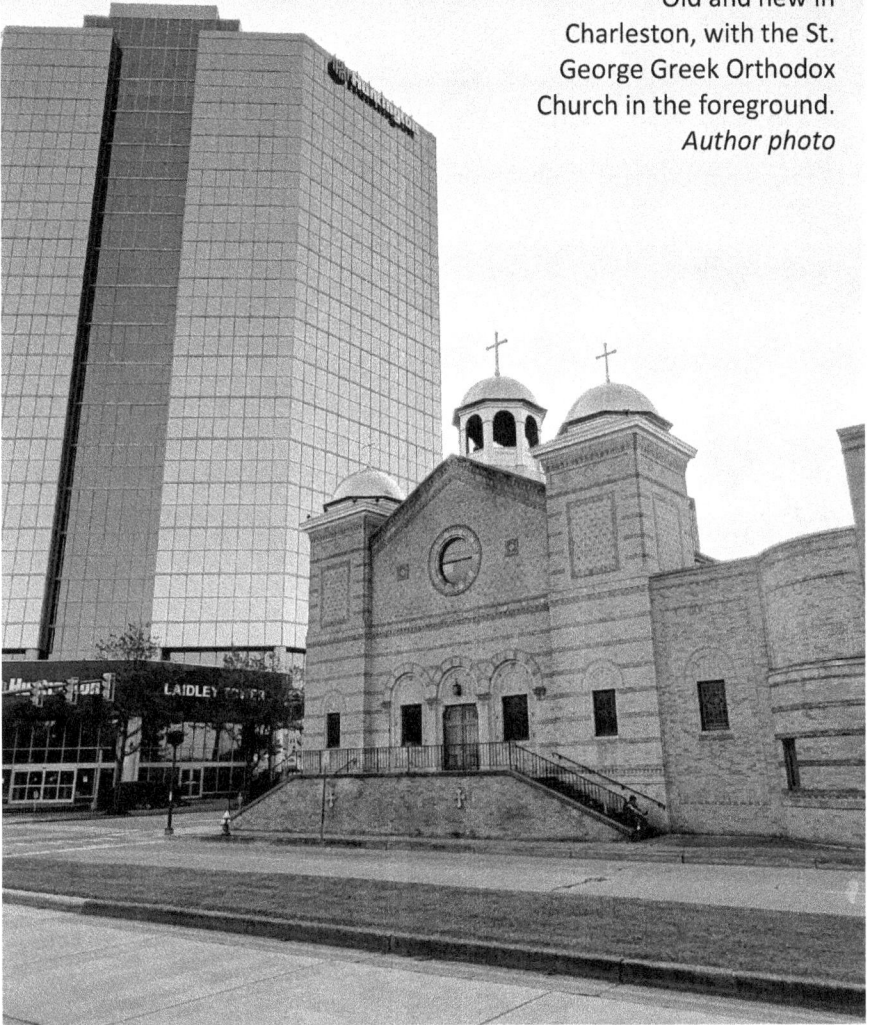

Old and new in Charleston, with the St. George Greek Orthodox Church in the foreground. *Author photo*

Ducks on a boat ramp at Daniel Boone State Park. *Author photos*

Looking at downtown on the Kanawha River. *Author photo*

References

"2 Leagues Merge for New Season," Chicago Tribune, sect. 2, p. 2, Feb. 7, 1965.

"20 Best Things to Do in Charleston, West Virginia," vacationidea.com, Oct. 14, 2021.

"1986-1989 Charleston Gunners," funwhileitlasted.net.

A&W and Painter's Drive-In ads, Charleston Daily Mail, p. 23, Sept. 30, 1966.

A&W ad, Charleston Daily Mail, p. 7B, Oct. 21, 1976.

"Airplane Leaves For North Pole," Charleston Daily Mail, p. 12, Nov. 18, 1934.

"Amazing Luna Park Photos," mywvhome.com.

"Amusements. Luna Park," Charleston Daily Mail, p. 4, July 27, 1914.

"Amusements. Luna Park," Charleston Daily Mail, p. 4, Aug. 21, 1914.

"The Arcade," mywvhome.com.

"Arrested Pair Admit Series Of Local Crimes," Charleston Daily Mail, p. 1, Oct. 4, 1960.

"Audiences' Taste Controls Profits," Charleston Daily Mail, p. 1, May 20, 1971.

"Auto Racing," wvencyclopedia.org.

"A.W. Cox Department Store in Hinton," wvnews.com, Aug. 13, 2019.

Barlett, Donald L. and Steele, James B. "How death came to a once-prosperous discount-store chain," inquirer.com, June 12, 2012.

"Barlows Skating Rink," mywvhome.com.

"BBF," columbusrestauranthistory.com.

"Between Fifty and Seventy-Five People Drowned Through Flood; Property Loss Huge; Relief Sent," Charleston Mail, p. 1, Aug. 11, 1916.

Bean Bros. ad, Charleston Daily Mail, p. 13, Aug. 24, 1933.

"Big Legion Dance Planned For Christmas," Hinton Daily News, p. 1, Dec. 12, 1946.

"Bill Barrett Dies At 55," Raleigh Register, p. 1, Nov. 14, 1977.

"Black Fury," imdb.com.

"Blaine Island," theclio.com, June 10,2021.

Boeck, Larry. "Hunsaker's No Cream Puff," Louisville Courier-Journal, Sports p. 12, Oct. 23, 1960.

"Board to Consider Cage Tourney Here," Charleston Daily Mail, p. 9, Dec. 5, 1934.

"Borden's Better Foods," cabellcountydoorstothepast.com.

Brown, Jimmy. "Clay Tests Hunsaker In Pro Debut Tonight," Louisville Courier-Journal, Sports p. 4, Oct. 29, 1960.

Brown, Jimmy. "Clay Wins 1st Fight As A Pro," Louisville Courier-Journal, p. 1, Oct. 30, 1960.

Bumgardner, Stan. "Charleston," Arcadia Publishing, 2006.

"Burger Boy Sign May Be Interfering With Aircraft," Raleigh Register, p. 1, March 11, 1964.

Burger Chef and Dairy Queen ads, Charleston Daily Mail, p. 21, March 14, 1966.

"Burglars Open Safe in Coyle's, Obtain $6,000," Charleston Daily Mail, p. 1, Sept. 13, 1960.

"The Bureaucracy Claims Yet Another Victim," Lexington Herald, p. D-12, March 3, 1978.

Callahan, James Morton. "History of West Virginia, Old and New, Volume 3," University of West Virginia, 1923.

Camp Drug ad, Charleston Daily Mail, p. 4, May 24, 1931.

"Cap Ferguson Hotel and Business Center," mywvhome.com.

"Casa Loma, 'Name' Band Stronghold, Being Razed," Charleston Daily Mail, p. 4, Jan. 6, 1952.

"Charleston," Hinton Daily News, p. 8, July 21, 1961.

"Charleston," wvencyclopedia.org.

"The Charleston Crime of the Century," mywvhome.com.

Charleston Motor Sales ad, Charleston Daily Mail, p. 11, Nov. 22, 1922.

"Charleston Park Burned," Hinton Independent-Herald, p. 5, May 15, 1940.

"Charleston Town Center," wvencyclopedia.org.

"Charleston TV Suspends Operation," Weirton Daily Times, p. 24, Feb. 3, 1955.

"Charleston Wins 82-7," Cumberland Evening Times, p. 14, Nov. 16, 1964.

"Charleston Wins Pennant," Owensboro (Ky.) Messenger-Inquirer, p. 3, Sept. 22, 1913.

"Charleston, W.Va., pulls itself up by bootstraps," Carlisle (Pa.) Sentinel, p. B8, June 4, 1984.

Chester's ad, Charleston Daily Mail, p. 15, Nov. 30, 1934.

"Chuck Yeager's Flight Under The South Side Bridge," mywvhome.com.

Cinematreasures.org.

"Clark Murder Offer Renewed," Raleigh Register, p. 1, July 15, 1959.

Concert ads, Sunday Gazette-Mail, p. 10S, March 5, 1972.

Concert ads, Sunday Gazette-Mail, p. 10S, Nov. 12, 1972.

Concertarchives.org.

"Concert Set," Raleigh Register, p. 2, March 20, 1975.

Connor, Charles. "Roving the Valley With Friends and Neighbors," Charleston Daily Mail, p. 4. Jan. 27, 1952.

Connor, Charlie. "City's Building Records Broken," Charleston Daily Mail, p. 13, Dec. 28, 1965.

"The Contest of the Century," mywvhome.com.

"Court Fines Girl, 19, Held in Rink Row," Charleston Daily Mail, p. 1, Feb. 2, 1967.

"Continental Basketball Association Eastern Division," La Crosse (Wis.) Tribune, p. 41, Nov. 30, 1986.

"Coyle & Richardson," mywvhome.com.

Cummings, Tom. "Kanawha Airport Landing Level Lower," Charleston Daily Mail, p. 9, Sept. 11, 1970.

"December 12, 1975: Original Shoney's in Charleston Closes," wvpublic.org, Dec. 12, 2019.

The Diamond ad, Charleston Daily Mail, p. 7, April 15, 1920.

"The Diamond," thedepartmentstoremuseum.org.

"The Diamond," mywvhome.com.

"Dream of Colored Man Being Worked Out Here," Charleston Daily Mail, sect. 2, p. 4, July 30, 1922.

"Drive-In Opened," Beckley Post-Herald, p. 6, May 22, 1963.

"Duck Saves Rooster From Drowning After Fall From Boat in Elk River," Charleston Daily Mail, p. 1, Jan. 29, 1933.

Earnest, Brian. "Car of the Week: 1937 Hudson Terraplane pickup," oldcarsweekly.com.

"East Bank and Barrackville Celebrate Hoop Titles," Raleigh Register, p. 6, March 26, 1956.

El Rancho ad, Sunday Gazette-Mail, p. 32P, Jan. 29, 1967.

"Elvis Presley Grosses $253,000 for 3 Concerts," Oakland Tribune, p. 20, July 17, 1975.

"Elvis Presley Third Show Now Sellout," Charleston Daily Mail, p. 5, March 25, 1975.

"Ex-Cons Caught Robbing School," Raleigh Register, p. 1, Oct. 3, 1960.

"Families in City Made Homeless," Charleston Daily Mail, p. 1, Jan. 24, 1935.

"Female Victims of Violence," U.S. Department of Justice, bjs.ojp.gov, Sept. 23, 2009.

Fields, Dan. "Seized Film Is Returned," Charleston Daily Mail, p. 8, July 17, 1969.

Fife Street Shoe Shop ad, Charleston Daily Mail, p. 5, Nov. 30, 1922.

Fife Street Shoe Shop ad, Sunday Gazette-Mail, p. 27E, Jan. 21, 1962.

"Fire Destroys Radio Station At Charleston," Hinton Leader, p. 1, Nov. 29, 1928.

"Flash Flood In Charleston, West Virginia – July, 1961," storiespodcast.net, July 20, 2021.

"Flood Damage Almost Erased from City's Garrison Ave.," Sunday Gazette-Mail, p. 30, Dec. 17, 1961.

"The Flood Of 1961," mywvhome.com.

"Flood Danger Growing Less As Cold Sets New Low of 7 Above," Charleston Daily Mail, p. 1, Jan. 25, 1935.

"For What It's Worth," cjablog.blogspot.com.

Fountain Hobby Center ad, Charleston Daily Mail, p. 11, Jan. 13, 1961.

Frazier, Allison and Womack, Kyle. "Stone & Thomas Building," theclio.com, July 4, 2020.

"From Rags to Riches," estepsthenulook.net, April 1989.

"Gangster Model Auto," Charleston Daily Mail, p. 10, Sept. 18, 1935.

Gould, Jerry. "Homeless Find Shelters In Charleston," Weirton Daily Times, p. 1, July 21, 1961.

"Governor's Gate Is Repossessed," Lebanon (Pa.) Daily News, p. 23, March 10, 1978.

Groceteria.com.

"The Massive West Virginia Blizzard Of January 1978 Will Never Be Forgotten," onlyinyourstate.com, Dec. 2, 2019.

Gwin, Adrian. "Arcade Remains Popular With Shoppers," Charleston Daily Mail, p. B1, July 20, 1976.

Gwin, Adrian. "End of an Institution," Charleston Daily Mail, p. B1, March 25, 1976.

Hager, Don. "Galaxy Of All-Stars Covers All Of KVC," Charleston Daily Mail, p. 1C, Dec. 13, 1973.

"Half-Million-Dollar Heck's Store Going Up," Charleston Daily Mail, p. 17, May 17, 1961.

Hardman, A.L. "Stennett Finally Convinced Them," Sunday Gazette-Mail, p. 2D, June 23, 1974.

Harold, Zack. "The Greatest's First Foe," wvliving.com, Spring 2019.

"Heck's" wvencyclopedia.org.

"Heck's Store Sale Plan Fails," Weirton Daily Times, p. 11, Jan. 15, 1969.

"History," ucwv.edu.

"History," woodrumsbuilding.com.

"The History of the Diamond Department Store," mywvhome.com.

"History of WCHS-TV, Charleston," jeff560.tripod.com.

"History of WOBU/WCHS Radio, Charleston," jeff560.tripod.com.

H.O. Baker Co. ad, Charleston Daily Mail, p. 3, May 9, 1932.

Horn, Hailey. "The Hotel Kanawha/Arcade Building," theclio.com, March 6, 2017.

"Hotel Kanawha," abandonedonline.net.

"Hotel Manager Takes Own Life," Charleston Daily Mail, p. 1, Sept. 1, 1933.

"Hot Line," Charleston Daily Mail, p. 8, Feb. 3, 1971.

"Hot Line," Charleston Daily Mail, p. 9, Jan. 11, 1973.

Humphrey, Harold. "Talents and Tunes on Music Machines," The Billboard, Jan. 31, 1942.

"Ice Sports, Inc., to Build Rink in Kanawha City," Charleston Daily Mail, p. B7, June 13, 1937.

"Increased Power Sought By WSAZ," Hinton Independent-Herald," p. 8, July 16, 1931.

"Is a Polygraph Test Admissible as Evidence?" hg.org.

"Jackson drafted again," Noblesville (Ind.) Ledger," p. 7, Aug. 12, 1986.

"Joseph McCarthy" (obituary), legacy.com.

"Just in Sport," Charleston Daily Mail, p. 8, Sept. 5, 1922.

"Kanawha City Spurting With Business Growth," Sunday Gazette-Mail, p. 2F, Jan. 30, 1972.

Kearse Theatre ad, Charleston Daily Mail, p. 7, Oct. 30, 1922.

Kearse Theatre National Register of Historic Places Inventory Nomination Form, npgallery.nps.gov.

"Kearse Theatre Marks Another Step Forward in Development of the City," Charleston Daily Mail, p. 12, Nov. 26, 1922.

King Rex ad, Charleston Daily Mail, p. 8, Aug. 11, 1914.

Kittle, Bob. "Skillful Thief Steals Rings Valued at $14,000," Charleston Daily Mail, p. 1, June 12, 1974.

Kittle, Bob. "Thought it was a prank," Charleston Daily Mail, p. 7, Nov. 28, 1975.

"LaBabe Corey And The Casa Loma," mywvhome.com.

Louis Armstrong ad, Sunday Gazette-Mail, p. 6D, July 10, 1960.

"Luna Park Reduced To Vast Ruin," Hinton Daily News, p. 1, May 5, 1923.

"Luna Park Transition," mywvhome.com.

"The Lyric Theater on Summers Street," mywvhome.com.

MacKay, Iain and Peyton, Billy Joe. "Haddad Riverfront Park (Levee)," theclip.com, May 15, 2021.

Memorial Day variety store closure ad, Charleston Daily Mail, p. 2, May 28, 1936.

Montgomery Ward ad, Rutland (Vt.) Daily Herald, p. 25, Aug. 10, 1983.

"Movie Withdrawn, Charges Dropped," Charleston Daily Mail, p. 7, Nov. 16, 1972.

"Music — As Written," The Billboard, Nov. 29, 1947.

"NAACP Official Promises Picketing Of Skating Rink," Charleston Daily Mail, p. 3, March 19, 1966.

"Negroes Buy Ferguson Hotel in Charleston," Hinton Daily News, p. 2, Feb. 25, 1924.

"New Building Boom Now Expected Here," Charleston Daily Mail, p. 7, Dec. 18, 1915.

"New Discount Drug Chain Tested in Market Trials," Sunday Gazette-Mail, p. 7B, Nov. 20, 1966.

"No Roadside Tables in Wayne?" Charleston Daily Mail, p. 4, Aug. 17, 1961.

Oberlan's ad, Charleston Daily Mail, p. B3, Aug. 6, 1933.

"Oliver gets Charleston post," Bangor Daily News, p. 15, July 29, 1986.

"On the Town, Sunday Gazette-Mail, p. 12S, Jan. 26, 1964.

"Orlando Plays Bulldogs For CFL Crown," Cumberland (Md.) Evening Times, p. 13, Nov. 28, 1966.

Owens Drive-In ad, Sunday Gazette-Mail, p. 11S, Jan. 6, 1974.

Owens Drive-In ad, Sunday Gazette-Mail, p. 7E, Oct. 30, 1977.

Paxton, Mark. "Downtown Concerned About Getting 'Malled'," Centre Daily Times (State College, Pa.)

p. 7, Nov. 7, 1983.

Peeks, Edward. "New Heck's Store Will Open Monday," Sunday Gazette-Mail, p. 1B, Nov. 6, 1977.

People's Store ad, Charleston Daily Mail, p. 2, June 24, 1931.

"Permit Obtained for New Coyle Structure," Charleston Daily Mail, p. 4, Nov. 27, 1922.

Peyton, Billy Joe. "Historic Charleston: The First 225 Years," HPNbooks, San Antonio.

Peyton, Billy Joe and Warmack, Kyle. "Union Carbide Corporation," theclio.com, Feb. 2, 2018.

"Historic Charleston: The First 225 Years," HPNbooks, San Antonio.

Piggly Wiggly ad, Charleston Daily Mail, p. 2, June 19, 1919.

"Point Pleasant-Gallipolis Team in V.V. League," Point Pleasant Register, p. 1, March 2, 1910.

"Pool To Integrate," Beckley Post-Herald, p. 7, July 1, 1967.

Powell, Bob. "WCHS," wvpublic.org.

Profootballarchives.com.

"Putnam Blaze Is Fatal," Beckley Post-Herald, p. 1, Nov, 28, 1975.

Putt-Putt ad, Sunday Gazette-Mail, p. 11C, June 28, 1959.

"Read the Charleston Gazette-Mail Story & Observations from the Authors," murderonstaunton.com.

"River Bridge Collapsed, 13 Known Dead," Chillicothe (Mo.) Constitution-Tribune, p. 1, July 26, 1926.

"Rock Lake Pool," cchs1959irish.com.

"Rock Lake Pool," mywvhome.com.

Rock Lake Pool ad, Charleston Daily Mail, p. 10, Aug. 2, 1933.

Rock Lake Pool ad, Charleston Daily Mail, p. 10, July 4, 1937.

"Rock Lake Pool Again Picketed; No Water Hosing," Beckley Post-Herald, p. 1, Aug. 8, 1965.

"Rock Lake Pool Owner Says Patrons Favor Segregation," Charleston Daily Mail, p. 6, July 21, 1964.

"Rockets Franchise In Jeopardy," Beckley Post-Herald, p. 20, Jan. 26, 1969.

"Rockets Streak By Rifles, 24-7, Capture CFL Crown," Raleigh Register, p. 8, Nov. 29, 1965.

Roller Derby ad, Charleston Daily Mail, p. 8, Jan. 16, 1970.

"The Roma Hotel Bombing of 1927," mywvhome.com.

"Seek Shelter for Homeless in Kanawha," Hinton Daily News, p. 1, July 21, 1961.

Setlist.fm.

Shindig! ad, Charleston Daily Mail, p. 27, April 30, 1965.

"Shot Fired at Ford — Woman is Seized," San Francisco Chronicle, p. 1, Sept. 22, 1975.

Sigler, Joe. "Economic Boycott Of Pool Requested," Charleston Daily Mail, p. 9, July 8, 1964.

"Skating Rink Closes Doors," Charleston Daily Mail, p. 10, June 1, 1967.

"Skating Tournament Starts Sunday Night," Charleston Daily Mail, p. 12, Aug. 26, 1916.

"Skyline Skeds 50-Lap Race," Raleigh Register, p. 8, Oct. 26, 1954.

Sleepy Jeffers ad, Shreveport Journal, p. 2D, Feb. 28, 1950.

"Snowstorm of January 1978," wvencyclopedia.org.

Spradling, Andrew. "Mineral Wells," andrewspradling.wordpress.com, Oct. 20, 2016.

Squires, M. Lynne. "Looking Back at the Libbey-Owens-Ford," charlestonhomeandliving.com.

Squires, M. Lynne. "Looking Back at the Quarrier Diner," charlestonhomeandliving.com.

"St. Albans Reaction Moves Playoff 100 Miles," Charleston Daily Mail, p. 9, Nov. 12, 1968.

"State Staggers Back to Normal as Record Early Storm Abates," Hinton Daily News, p. 1,
     Nov. 27, 1950.

Statscrew.com.

Steelhammer, Rick. "Flood of 1916," wvencyclopedia.org, March 14, 2018.

"Stewart's Original Hot Dogs 'The Little Orange Drive-In That Could," stwewartshotdogs.com
     (cached).

Stover, Dorothy. "Long-standing West Side business gets modern makeover,"
        wvgazette66.rissing.com, Sept. 7, 2015.

Strand ad, Charleston Daily Mail, p. 8, Feb. 6, 1925.

The Strand Cash Market ad, Charleston Daily Mail, p. 8, Sept. 1, 1916.

"Summers to be a Second Broadway When Completed," Charleston Daily Mail, p. 24, Aug. 6, 1922.

Tag Galyean Rambler ad, Charleston Daily Mail, p. 8, Dec. 30, 1967.

Tall Fashions ad, Charleston Daily Mail, p. 29, Nov. 10, 1957.

"Teacher and Pupils of Decota School, Forced to Stand as Men Fire," Charleston Daily Mail,
        mywvhome.com.

"The Seeking Heart," tvguide.com.

"Today's World," Raleigh Register, p. 1, Sept. 13, 1966.

"Toledo Scores First UFL Win," Fremont (Ohio) News-Messenger, p. 20, Sept. 8, 1964.

"Tommy Dorsey Catalog 1941," colorado.edu.

Toren, J. Richard. "How Charleston Rockets Were Launched," Raleigh Register, p. 15, May 28, 1964.

"Trail Drive In," mywvhome.com

Tribe, Ivan M. "Mountaineer Jamboree: Country Music in West Virginia," University Press of Kentucky,
        1984.

Trivillian's ad, Charleston Daily Mail, Feb. 16, 1951.

Tucker, Jill. "Kenneth Iacovoni — special agent," sfgate.com, Oct. 29, 2006.

"TV Jockey Profile: Record Hop Starring Dick Reid," Billboard Music Week, p. 35, March 27, 1961.

"Unsolved: The Murder of Juliet Staunton Clark," Mysterious WV, youtube.com.

Vacation Dance Party ad, Sunday Gazette-Mail, p. 11C, June 21, 1959.

Waters, J. "The Daniel Boone Hotel," mywvhome.com.

Waters, J. "The Fife Street Shoe Shop," mywvhome.com.

Waters, J. "The Firestone Store," mywvhome.com.

Waters, J. "The Frontier Drive In Theater 1954," mywvhome.com.

Waters, J. "Pure Oil Refinery At Cabin Creek," mywvhome.com.

Waters, J. "Quarrier Diner," mywvhome.com.

Waters, J. "Quarrier Street 1930s," mywvhome.com.

Waters, J. "Some Area Gas Stations," mywvhome.com.

Waters, J. "Stewarts Root Beer," mywvhome.com.

Waters, J. "Totten's Service Station," mywvhome.com.

"Wertz Airfield — Campus History and Community, WVSU Archives & Special Collections,"
        library.wvstateu.edu.

"Whole Families are Missing," Clarksburg Daily Telegram, p. 1, Aug. 11, 1916.

Widmeyer, Scott. "Woman Top Grad Of Welding School," Charleston Daily Mail, p. 2, May 15, 1975.

"Wilt Tallies 41 For New Record," Chambersburg Public Opinion, p. 10, Feb, 15, 1966.

"Won't Bother TV Again," Beckley Post-Herald, p. 7, March 18, 1964.

WKNA programming schedule, Charleston Daily Mail, p. 6, April 25, 1954.

"WKNA-TV Channel 49 (ABC, Ind.)," geocities/radiojunkie1 (archived).

Woodrums ad, Sunday Gazette-Mail, p. 3L, Feb. 23, 1975.

"WV Broadcasting Hall of Fame," mrtvw.org.

"WV - Juliet 'Julia' Staunton Clark, 59, Charleston, 21 August 1953," websleuths.com.

Young Rascals ad, Charleston Daily Mail, p. 17, Nov. 15, 1967.

Young's Department Store ad, Charleston Daily Mail, p. 13, Nov. 1, 1963.

Capitol Street in
1973, above, and
2021, left. Harry
*Schaefer,
National Archives,
and author photo*

CHARLESTON CENTURY

Also by the author

Historical nonfiction

Yesterday's Highways

America's First Highways

Highways of the South

The Great American Shopping Experience

Martinsville Memories

Huntington Century

Fresno Growing Up

Fresno Century

Roanoke Century

San Luis Obispo Century

Danville Century

Cambria Century

Highway 99: The History of California's Main Street

Highway 101: The History of El Camino Real

The Legend of Molly Bolin

A Whole Different League

Please Stop Saying That!

Fiction

The Talismans of Time

Pathfinder of Destiny

Nightmare's Eve

Death's Doorstep

Memortality

Paralucidity
The Only Dragon
Identity Break
Feathercap

STEPHEN H. PROVOST

Praise for other works

"If you have any interest in highways, old diners and motels and such, or 20th century US history, this book is for you. It is without a doubt one of the best highway books ever published."

— Dan R. Young, founder OLD HIGHWAY 101 group, on **Yesterday's Highways**

"Profusely illustrated throughout, **Highway 99** is unreservedly recommended as an essential and core addition to every community and academic library's California History collections."

— California Bookwatch

"… an engaging narrative that pulls the reader into the story and onto the road. … I highly recommend **Highway 99: The History of California's Main Street**, whether you're a roadside archaeology nut or just someone who enjoys a ripping story peppered with vintage photographs."

— Barbara Gossett,
Society for Commercial Archaeology Journal

"The genres in this volume span horror, fantasy, and science-fiction, and each is handled deftly. … **Nightmare's Eve** should be on your reading list. The stories are at the intersection of nightmare and lucid dreaming, up ahead a signpost … next stop, your reading pile. Keep the nightlight on."

— R.B. Payne, Cemetery Dance

"As informed and informative as it is entertaining and absorbing, **Fresno Growing Up** is very highly recommended for personal, community, and academic library 20th Century American History collections."

— John Burroughs, Reviewer's Bookwatch

"An essential primer for anyone seeking an entrée into the genre. Provost serves up a smorgasbord of highlights gleaned from his personal memories of and research into the various nooks and crannies of what 'used-to-be' in professional team sports."

— Tim Hanlon, Good Seats Still Available,
on **A Whole Different League**

"The complex idea of mixing morality and mortality is a fresh twist on the human condition. ... **Memortality** is one of those books that will incite more questions than it answers. And for fandom, that's a good thing."

— Ricky L. Brown, Amazing Stories

"Punchy and fast paced, **Memortality** reads like a graphic novel. ... (Provost's) style makes the trippy landscapes and mind-bending plot points more believable and adds a thrilling edge to this vivid crossover fantasy."

— Foreword Reviews

"**Memortality** by Stephen Provost is a highly original, thrilling novel unlike anything else out there."

— David McAfee, bestselling author of
33 A.D., 61 A.D., and 79 A.D.

"Provost sticks mostly to the classics: vampires, ghosts, aliens, and even dragons. But trekking familiar terrain allows the author to subvert readers' expectations. ... Provost's poetry skillfully displays the same somber themes as the stories. ... Worthy tales that prove external forces are no more terrifying than what's inside people's heads."

— Kirkus Reviews on **Nightmare's Eve**

About the author

Stephen H. Provost is the author of several books on 20th century America, covering topics that range from his hometown to department stores and shopping centers; from pop music and sports icons to the history of our nation's highways. During a 30-year career in journalism, he worked as a managing editor, sports editor, copy desk chief, columnist and reporter at five newspapers. As a novelist, he has written about dragons, mutant superheroes, and things that go bump in the night. A California native, he now lives in Virginia.

Did you enjoy this book?

Recommend it to a friend. And please consider rating it and/or leaving a brief review online at Amazon, Barnes & Noble and Goodreads.

www.ingramcontent.com/pod-product-compliance
Lightning Source LLC
Chambersburg PA
CBHW070329090426
42733CB00012B/2415